MODERN WEIGHT-TRAINING

Leaving for the Mexico Olympic Games.
From left to right: Wally Holland, Secretary B.A.W.L.A., Assistant Secretary International Weight Lifters' Federation, Olympic Team Manager; Alistair Murray, National and Olympic Coach for Great Britain and now National and Olympic Coaching Adviser; Louis Martin, M.B.E., World Weightlifting Champion, British and Commonwealth Games Champion.

MODERN WEIGHT-TRAINING

The Key to Physical Power

ALISTAIR MURRAY, M.S.R.G.
Britain's National Weightlifting Coach
to the B.A.W.L.A. 1948-1971 and National and
Olympic Coaching Adviser

WITH 150 PHOTOGRAPHS: DIAGRAMS AND CHARTS

KAYE & WARD
LONDON

A. S. BARNES & CO
NEW YORK AND SOUTH BRUNSWICK

First published by
Nicholas Kaye Limited
1963
2nd edition published by
Kaye and Ward Limited
1971
Reprinted 1972, 1976

ISBN 0 7182 0868 4 (U.K.)

First American Edition 1971
Reprinted 1972, 1976
A. S. Barnes and Co., Inc.
Cranbury, N.J. 08512

Library of Congress Catalogue Card No. 71-114991

ISBN 0-498-07681-4 (U.S.A.)

Printed in the U.S.A.

CONTENTS

		Page
Foreword by Oscar State	. . . .	6
Introduction	. . . . . .	8
1 Weight-training and its Variations	. . .	12
2 Kinesiology	. . . . . .	18
3 Anatomy Simplified	. . . . .	33
4 Breathing	. . . . . .	44
5 Weight-training Terms	. . . .	46
6 Schedule Construction	. . . .	49
7 Variation of Schedules to Alter Results	. .	53
8 The Principles of Body Mechanics and Athletics	.	57
9 Weight-training and its Adaptation to Athletics	.	62
10 Isometric Muscle Work	. . .	64
11 Training for Strength, Power and Speed	. .	68
12 Weight-training Equipment	. . .	70
13 Major Weight-training Exercises	. .	72

FOREWORD

By OSCAR STATE (general secretary of the International Weightlifting Federation and British Empire & Commonwealth Weightlifting Council)

IT is accepted in the world of weightlifting that Al Murray is one of the greatest coaches, particularly in the field of scientific Olympic lifting.

Al Murray's career began with winning Scottish championships and British records. During the war he showed his flair for coaching when, as a Warrant Officer in the A.P.T.C., he trained over 300 assistant P.T.I.'s and was also a member of the A.A. Command Gymnastic Team. For his exceptional work in introducing weight-training with 'ack-ack' shells for gun crews he was awarded the Meritorious Certificate for Outstanding Service and Devotion to Duty.

After the war, he qualified as a hospital remedial gymnast under the Ministry of Health and the Ling Physical Education Association. These outstanding qualifications decided me in 1948 to secure his appointment as Britain's first-ever National Weightlifting Coach and he has held that position ever since. In this capacity he has trained hundreds of club coaches and travelled extensively throughout Britain lecturing and coaching at universities, colleges, Service units, schools and youth centres.

His reputation quickly spread abroad and he received invitations to coach in Ireland, Switzerland, Holland, Germany, Norway, Iran, the Philippines. He is still technical adviser to the Swiss and German Federations and his training tours have so far taken him to twelve European countries. As National Coach he has travelled with British teams to World and European championships, Regional, Empire and Olympic Games.

Today Al Murray is regularly consulted by sports governing bodies for weight-training advice, among them the Lawn Tennis Association for whom he helped Shirley Bloomer and Angela Buxton to reach top ranking. The Amateur Athletic Association encouraged such stars as Gordon Pirie, Peter Hildreth, Martin Lucking to go to him for personal coaching. Both Oxford and Cambridge University rowing crews enjoyed his intensive weight-training sessions. He has also worked with the L.C.C., Royal Navy and Royal Air Force and the Amateur Swimming Association (in conjunction with Bert Kinnear).

When Al Murray's contract with the Ministry of Education ended, he became a director of George Grose Ltd besides forming his own company which deals with his teaching, coaching and personal appearances on television, etc.

Though the majority of his work has been with sports governing bodies, he still finds time to run personal classes, not just for athletes but for men and women from all walks of life—Peter Sellers, Victor Sylvester, Max Wall and Eartha Kitt are among those he has advised.

Al Murray recently notched two further successes. He was coach of the British team when Louis Martin of Jamaica and England won his 1962 world championship in Budapest; then Al was chosen as coach to the England weightlifting team for the Empire Games in Australia the same year. The ten-man team returned with nine medals—four Gold, two Silver and three Bronze.

The aforementioned took place during his first fifteen years as National Coach, up until 1963. By then his services were in even greater demand throughout Europe, not only in Olympic lifting but in the widest sense of physical education and exercise therapy.

The 1968 Olympics in Mexico brought his Olympic participation up to five Games in series. In his twenty-one years as National Coach he has coached at dozens of World, International and British Commonwealth Championships.

During all this time his interest in the academic and medical side of exercise had continued to grow and in 1965, inspired by Dr Harold Lewis (an eminent physiologist), he opened the City Gym and Health Clinic for business executives, right by the side of St Pauls Cathedral, in the City of London.

In the early summer of 1970, after four and a half years of such empirical research into 'executive' health and cardiac rehabilitation, official research began in that Gym. This has involved many leading medical researchers, in conjunction with Al Murray who are participating in research at national level. His City businessmen and their work in this field is now known and respected throughout the World.

This book brings to you some of his vast and varied knowledge in the fields of weight-training and weightlifting. I am sure that sportsmen of all kinds will benefit from the advice so clearly and concisely presented here.

INTRODUCTION

By the time you get to the end of this book, you will at least have learnt something of my knowledge of weight-training. Unfortunately, it doesn't work both ways. For all I know, you may be a regular weightlifter, an advanced coach or even a champion. On the other hand, you might never have lifted a barbell in your life.

You see my dilemma—I cannot write individually for every grade of weight-trainer. So, I have decided that you, the reader, can be any one of the above and the book will start from scratch.

Those of you who have some experience will certainly recognize most of the instruction but I have tried to approach every subject, whether elementary or advanced, from a fresh angle. In this way, I think, it will cater for every weight-trainer and instructor.

Before we get down to the meat of the subject, perhaps you should know something about the development of weight-training.

The desire to lift great weights has been in man for a long time, but the organization of this urge into a competitive sport has all taken place in this century. In recent years strength has been given great significance by the Iron Curtain countries in an attempt to symbolize their supremacy. An example of this is the publicity and importance they attach to their weightlifting champions, especially their present world heavyweight champion, Yuri Vlasov, who is known as the 'World's Strongest Man'.

Up to the 1920s, much of the inspiration for lifting great weights came from the professional strong men, the Sandows, the Cyclops and the Saxons of the circus, stage and fairground. These men were certainly strong but most of them had not been born strong as the public then imagined; they had just trained hard as the modern weight-trainer does.

These showmen specialized mainly with spectacular equipment like iron-bars, 'unbreakable' chains and the like. It was their emulators who turned to more conventional equipment. They started training with solid barbells and dumb-bells.

The next stage came when the barbells and dumb-bells were hollowed and loaded with varying amounts of shot. This meant the weights could be adjusted to suit the lifter, but you can imagine how long and tedious the job must have been.

The big, big break came when disc-loaded barbells and dumb-bells were introduced, similar to the modern ones. At last, weights could be adjusted to within a few pounds in seconds. Weightlifting competitions were already in vogue, but these were usually thrown open to all body weights so you had the bantamweights competing with the heavyweight on equal terms—and may the best man win. It wasn't till later that class weights limited lifters to competing against rivals of their own weight group.

Lifts in those days (and there were as many as 44 listed at one time by the British Amateur Weightlifters' Association) were based on movements which needed little or no speed. It was mainly strength, balance and technique that were needed then.

The air was cleared with the introduction of the three recognized Olympic lifts:

The Two-Hands Clean and Press.
The Two-Hands Snatch,
The Two-Hands Clean and Jerk.

I look upon this as the other great step forward in producing competition for the athletic strongman, as opposed to the professional strongman with his slow-moving feats of sheer strength. The three Olympic lifts demand all the physical and mental qualities that the true athlete must have.

Physique competitions took hold in the 1930s but they had little effect then on the world of weightlifting. The main aim of those early bodybuilders was still to become really strong men. Most enthusiasts had a healthy interest in breaking weightlifting records.

Strength, though, took second place after World War II when the Americans set the pace. The United States became 'physique mad'. A 'body beautiful' became a national status symbol and in many cases physiques were developed far beyond their corresponding strength. Full-scale competitions were held with tremendous money prizes being offered to attract the musclemen. The prize went to the man with the finest physique and not to the strongest competitor. Appearance overruled functional efficiency.

Someone called these men 'people who had muscles in places where other people don't have places.' He wasn't far wrong.

This craze spread to Britain, and the exaggerated behaviour of a very small minority turned the public against weight-training in most of its forms, and against weightlifting as a competitive sport. And true physical education specialists looked down on this cult of 'muscles at any price' as much as the public did.

The value of weight-training with a purpose was brought out during the War. When in 1943 Ack-Ack Command introduced a new high-speed mechanical loader for their guns but found to their horror that the gun crews were not strong enough to keep the loader supplied with heavy shells, I was called in from the Army Physical Training Corps to see if I could help.

I decided to put a squad of gunners through a special session of progressive resistance training using 48 lb. shells. The training lasted six weeks. At the end of it the boys were more than able to match the loader's appetite.

It was important that the results were witnessed not only by the Army authorities but also by many physical training instructors. I think this was the point when weightlifting was accepted, at least by the important few, as an aid to strength and physical efficiency rather then to appearance.

This was only a start, though, and the public still had to be convinced. Happily, the situation was greatly improved by Oscar State, then secretary of the British Amateur Weightlifters' Association. He enlisted my help as B.A.W.L.A.'s first National Coach in 1948 and together we drew up the first ever-weight-training schedules. Geoff Dyson, who at the time was the A.A.A's National Coach, fully suppported these schedules for his athletes and the results spoke for themselves.

Our first 'guinea pig', incidentally, was shot-putter John Savidge. Weight-training increased his bodyweight by three stone (42 lb.) and played a great part in improving his putting distances.

Swimming quickly followed the lead and it was Bert Kinnear, as National Swimming Coach, who introduced weight-training schedules for the swimmers. Today there are few sports that don't benefit from weight-training, fewer still which couldn't.

After leaving the Army, I qualified as a remedial gymnast, but as National Coach I was able to continue spending part of my time analysing the mechanics of the three Olympic lifts. The remainder of my time was taken up by the work of training instructors in all branches of weight-training and lifting.

Eventually education authorities changed their whole attitude to weight-training. Photographs began to appear regularly in the papers showing our top sportsmen training with weights. The image of oiled, bronzed musclemen on beaches was disappearing fast from the public's eye. And nothing helped so much as the results those sports-men had achieved with their weights, especially such men as Gordon Pirie and Arthur Rowe.

Some of the atheletes mentioned have long since passed their prime in competition, but were discussed because they were amongst the pioneers who used weight training to good advantage.

My aim in writing this book is to ensure that it lives up to its title and provides you with the latest information possible.

I hope it will be of help to you whether you teach, coach, lift or train with weights.

CHAPTER 1

WEIGHT-TRAINING AND ITS VARIATIONS

1. AS A MEANS TO PHYSICAL IMPROVEMENT

Free standing exercises (or exercises without apparatus) have been practised for a long time to keep the individual healthy, to mobilize the joints, and to some degree improve development.

Many years ago it was found that to improve the size or power of a muscle, it must be exercised against progressive resistance. The resistance needed to be a known amount and one which could be varied easily—hence the arrival of modern weights and equipment.

The objective of most weight-trainers today is to develop their physical well-being. Basically, this is achieved by practising various exercises, each one designed to develop a particular part of the body. These exercises are very simple and they are repeated by the individual ten or twelve times. They have become known as *repetitions*. By the end of a programme nearly every muscle in the body will have been exercised. The number of repetitions performed depends on the aim of the individual, but in the early days, ten to twelve is sufficient.

In this form of weight-training, it isn't necessary to have more than three sessions a week. Even two sessions a week will bring considerable improvement. This is training for physical improvement in its simplest form. It is ideal for the business man, or woman, to keep toned up because after the training session they can put their barbell away and completely forget about it until the next session.

I mention this so that no one gets the impression that this standard of weight-training is going to take up all his time and dominate his life. Not a bit of it. In fact one England footballer brought himself back to match fitness after an accident by using his weights only during television commercials!

For the next stage, we go to the young man or woman who wants to develop a physique more impressive than that of the normal person. Alternatively, they might be concerned about a flabby figure brought about by an inactive way of life. They need only carry out two sessions a week, but the sessions should be longer, and their repetitions and sets vary from those of the beginner or from the simple system mentioned above.

They might then decide that having developed a fine physique, they would like to enter competitions, so well and good; it is a natural desire. But the next step I just cannot condone is when an individual becomes obsessed with the idea of developing every fibre of his body to the maximum. What he eats, when he sleeps, what he should do and should not do is worked out microscopically to the exclusion of all else. He might pose for hours for 'beefcake' photographs. All this can reach such proportions that the outside world is pushed into the background as he strives to produce the ultimate in physique, without consideration for the other physical and mental qualities.

To some this attitude of mind might develop into an unhealthy form of weight-training. The most that can be said for it is that it is better than many other activities which are actually detrimental to the community.

The difference between the man who is interested in the efficiency of his physique rather than its appearance might be hard to recognize, and this might seem a fine point to you, but I assure you it isn't. Weight-training produces fast and spectacular results. So you can see how easy it is for the young man engaged in physique competition to be swept on to the 'beefcake' stage.

One of the finest examples of a functional physique in this country is that of Rube Martin. He is a true athlete, an ex-British weight-lifting champion and an excellent gymnast. His pupils have followed his fine example and are being taught to appreciate the value of physical efficiency as well as that of impressive physique. I only hope you will do the same.

I have found that the exerciser's personality often shows itself after he has been training for a short while. And it is a sure guide to the branch of weight-training to which he will go on.

If shy, reserved or non-athletic, he will probably be more inclined to specialize in physique building. On the other hand, the athletically minded may go through a fierce spell of body-building and then find it increasingly difficult to resist the appeal of competitive Olympic weightlifting. The latter may find with practice, that although he has the competitive spirit, he lacks the speed, balance and co-ordination needed for Olympic weightlifting, in which case he can still express himself by training to break divisional or British lifting records on the many lifts that do not require the greater physical prowess of the three Olympic lifts. Finally, the person who finds he cannot devote the time needed to train for competitive lifting can still build fine health and a fine physique through regular weight-training.

2. AS AN AID TO REHABILITATION

Rehabilitation of patients by the use of resistance is far from new. For many years, the resistance was a weighted sandbag attached to a rope and pulley. Since World War II, small adjustable barbells, dumb-bells and legbells have come into increasingly common use as doctors, physiotherapists and remedial gymnasts realize their value.

Weights have their greatest value when a patient is discharged. He or she is able to buy a small barbell set and begin home training as in the early stages of Section 1. You would be surprised at the number of patients who aren't satisfied simply to return to normal health! Impressed by the rapid improvement they made with their weights in hospital, some even continue to progress up to competition standard.

Semi-paralysed people have also taken to weight-training and found it a great help, although many are unable to use all their limbs. Some even break records on lifts which do not require the activation of the injured or disabled part of the body.

I think there is great scope for this form of training in the cure or improvement of an inferiority complex. I have worked with patients during my years as a remedial gymnast in the Bridge of Earn Rehabilitation Centre who hardly dare look you in the eye. The cares of the whole world seem to be on their shoulders. Often their physical health is also impaired. We found weight-training the finest remedy for them.

After a few weeks, as they worked up to 50 and 60 lb. weights, they could look back at their first week when they had difficulty with a 10 lb. barbell. It is this opportunity to actually *measure* an improvement for which unconsciously they have been looking. I have seen remarkable changes take place in a man's nature in this way. It isn't just the body that improves: the whole mental attitude to face life is developed as well.

Where progressive resistance is required to improve the state of injured or defective muscles, no quicker method is known than weight-training to bring the patient back to normal fitness.

3. AS AN AID TO THE ATHLETE

The improved results of athletes who have trained with weights has done most to raise the status of this particular field. Yet Oscar State,

Geoff Dyson and I often laugh when we look back at those days in 1948 when athletes were gingerly trying out our schedules, using 25 lb. barbells and wondering if all that weight was going to slow them down and make them muscle-bound!

What a contrast is presented by the picture today when athletes like Arthur Rowe, Martyn Lucking and Vasiliy Rudyenkov and a host of others use weights up to and exceeding the 500 lb. mark for squatting and taking something like 285 lb. to their shoulders and then heave it to arms' length above their heads several times in succession.

Once the first results came in, the idea of weight-training for athletes spread like wildfire. Our struggle had not been to increase the weights these athletes used, but to get the idea accepted in the first place.

Other sports weren't slow to realize the potential that weight-training offered. The Amateur Athletic Association, the Amateur Swimming Association and the Lawn Tennis Association quickly recognized its value and we have reached such sports as rowing, football, boxing and rugby and many others. There are two big problems existing on the sporting side which I am being repeatedly asked to solve. First: how can weight-training be adapted to suit the special needs of sports which differ widely in their mechanics of movement? Second: how can the sportsmen know in what proportion he should mix his competitive training with his weight-training? I will answer these queries later in the book.

Some damage was done in the early days by coaches who let their enthusiasm run away with them, putting their pupils through such tough schedules that they were left with insufficient strength and energy for the specialized training required by their own event. Let me establish now that a sportsman must spend *most* of his time training for his particular event. But the *right amount* of weight-training can make a vast difference to his performance.

That amount is governed by the individual, by his event and by the position of the competitive season. Let me give you an extreme example of heavy weight-training during an athletics season.

In September 1961, I returned from a tour of Spain and was at once called in by the A.A.A. They had a problem. The Russian athletic team, having just arrived for a fixture against Great Britain at the White City, were asking for somewhere to train with their weights. Could I help?

I could. I invited them down to my small gymnasium at Wood

Green where they went through a strenuous schedule though it was only two days before the athletics match. When the session finished, their Olympic hammer champion Vasiliy Rudyenkov promised he would call on me again the day after the match to show me what weightlifting really meant to him.

As good as his word, he arrived at my main gymnasium in Fleet Street and started warming up. There was no sense of 'showing off' about this demonstration. It was just that having heard I was our Olympic weightlifting coach, he assumed I would be interested to see his performance. I was. In fact 'interested' wasn't the word for it.

As I stood there, I saw him press 305 lb., then reach 300 lb. with the highly skilful Two Hand Snatch, and finish with 375 lb. Clean and Jerk at his final attempt. Had Rudyenkov produced these figures in the World Weightlifting Championships at Vienna a few weeks later, he would have come fifth in the heavyweight class!

These lifts would be excellent for an Olympic weightlifter; for a hammer-thrower they are phenomenal; but for a hammer-thrower slap bang in the middle of his season—well, frankly I was astonished. But Vasiliy told me afterwards that it was not uncommon for Russian field athletic men to tackle weights in this way.

Of course, the field event athlete can continue with his weight-training long after the track man has begun to cut down on his, but Rudyenkov's performance at least showed how the two forms of training can be effectively combined.

4. OLYMPIC WEIGHTLIFTING

This, in a way, is the glamorous and athletic side of the world of weights, but, as you can imagine, with lifters from over eighty nations competing it is pretty tough getting to the top and tougher still staying there.

In an Olympic competition, the competitor has three attempts at each of the two Olympic lifts. His best lift at each is recorded and the lifter with the highest total is the winner. Today, there are eight bodyweight classes: Bantamweight—Featherweight—Lightweight—Middleweight — Light-heavyweight — Middle-heavyweight — Heavyweight and Super Heavyweight.

Weightlifters break their class records with almost monotonous regularity. Each time we feel the ultimate has been reached, but a new 'ultimate' soon arrives on the scene. The reason is that techniques and training methods are improving all the time and we are getting fresh and better material into the sport.

1.—Al Murray assists Louis Martin immediately after Martin had broken the middle-heavy-weight world record total and thus regained the World Championship—Budapest, 1962.

2.—Yuri Vlasov, former Russian World and Olympic Heavyweight Weightlifting champion. No mere muscleman, Vlasov speaks fluent French and studies aeronautical engineering at a Russian University.

3.—The Early Days. Geoff Dyson works with Al Murray on the construction of training schedules for his athletes.

4.—THE International Olympic Barbell.

5.—Squat Stand.

6.—Leg Pressing Machine.

7.—Leg Pressing Machine.

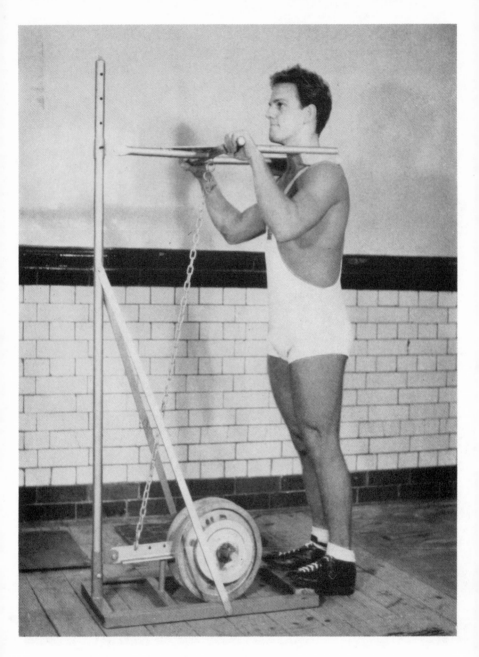

8.—Calf Machine.

9.—Calf Machine.

10.—Adjustable Long Inclined Bench.

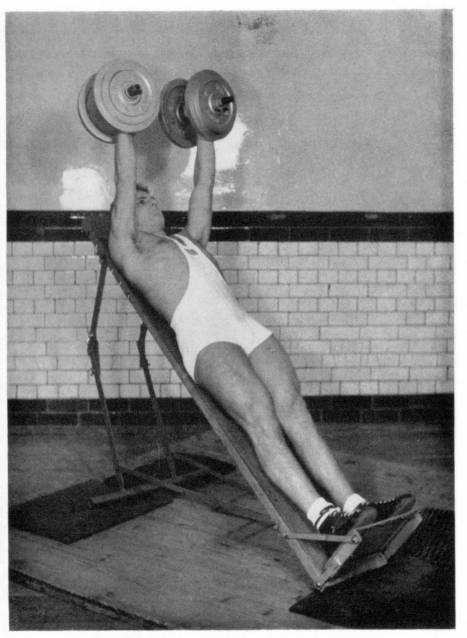

11.—Adjustable Long Inclined Bench in use with dumb-bells.

12.—Exceptional physiques are possible with weight-training. This is the American, Lud Schusterich.

13.—Powerful leg and hip extensors are needed for the explosive take-off and drive in the sprints.

14.—Al Murray talks to Doug Hepburn, whom he coaches, persuading him to continue a competition in Stockholm, Sweden, which he went on to win and became World Champion.

15.—The Australian Margaret Court has reached the top in lawn tennis with power and fitness that has never been seen in the women's game before. Hours of weight-training at Frank Sedgman's gymnasium has brought her success.

16.—(Left) Ted Aston with John Grimek (centre) former Mr Universe who will always be remembered as one of the great physiques—and Al Murray (right).

17.—Ian MacDonald Smith, Gold Medal winner at the 1968 Olympics, lying out to the fore of the picture, works out regularly in Al Murray's City Gym.

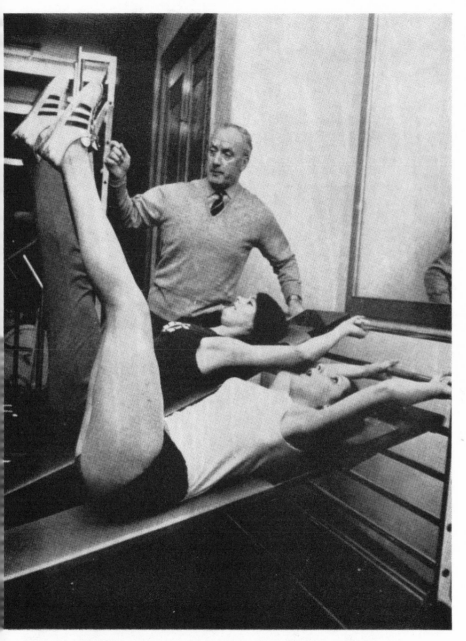

18.—Al Murray at his City Gym with two of Britain's best female high-jumpers, Linda Knowles (left) and Janet Oldall.

19.—Russia's hammer thrower Vasiliy Rudyenkov demonstrates his lifting capacities before Al Murray. The poundage on the barbell is 375 lb. Others in the picture are (left to right):—

Martyn Lucking,
Arthur Rowe and
Howard Payne.

20.—A photograph showing that to be a weightlifting champion you don't have to look any different from the man in the street. Here are Kurynov and Vlasov, champions from Russia.

The Olympic weightlifter today must train not only for a high degree of physical and mental fitness; but he must find the quickest route to maximum strength. He must always be trying to perfect his technique—a technique that will produce the most efficient way to lift the heaviest weights. He must do special exercises to improve his strength, co-ordination, speed, balance and explosiveness.

If you think that this is a pretty tall order, think of Vasiliy Rudyenkov. He did all that and still found time to become the world's best hammer-thrower.

A case in point was Gary Gubner's performances in the 1962 season in which he finished near the top of both world shot-putting *and* weightlifting. This proved that competitive weightlifting and 'heavy' athletics really can go hand-in-hand. Since the days of athletic success of men like Rudyenkov and Gubner, the names of those now using weight training to achieve their athletic ambitions have been too numerous to mention.

CHAPTER 2

KINESIOLOGY

The study of body mechanics (kinesiology) is the study of complex muscular movements. Unless the basic principles of kinesiology are understood, then body mechanics cannot be appreciated. This chapter aims to present the fundamentals of the subject so that the terms and movements described in later chapters can more readily be accepted.

Muscles are built up of hair-like fibres which are activated by the nervous system either to shorten, lengthen or hold a fixed position. It is these three actions that concern us mainly in this chapter and I list them here:

MUSCLE WORK

(a) Concentric

A muscle is working concentrically when it is actively shortening against resistance. When the body, or parts of the body, are to be raised or when outside resistance has to be overcome, the muscles involved are working concentrically.

Examples: Raising the body from the Squat, raising the arms above the head from the sideways position or raising the trunk from the sideways position or raising the trunk from the lying position into a sitting position, raising one leg, whilst standing. All raising movements. Exceptions: downward pulls on pulley machines or chest expanders.

(b) Eccentric

A muscle is working eccentrically when it is actively lengthening to permit the controlled lowering of the body, part of the body or some outside resistance.

Examples: Lowering the arms to the side from above the head or lowering any weight from any height or position.

Exception to this occurs when the lowering exceeds the speed of gravity. In other words, if the arms are pulled down from shoulder level to slap the thighs, the muscles are no longer working eccentrically. In fact, this action is produced by other muscles working concentrically.

(c) Static

A muscle is working statically when it is employed to hold a fixed position.

Example: If you stop during any movement, then the muscle used to hold that position is working statically. By merely standing to attention, the postural muscles are working statically.

These three classes of muscle work are also known by the terms *isotonic* and *isometric.* These two words have suddenly come into vogue in American sports weight-training manuals, yet in fact they are old-fashioned terms that have been in use since the beginning of the century.

Isotonic muscle work is the same as *Concentric* and *Eccentric.* *Isometric* is another term for *Static work.*

MUSCLE ACTION

Muscles work in the three different ways shown above. The muscles can also *act* for particular movements and for this reason they are given these group names:

(a) Prime Movers

The muscles responsible for *producing* concentric and permitting eccentric muscle work are known as the prime movers.

Example: When the arms are raised sideways, the abductors of the shoulders (or deltoids) are acting concentrically as the prime movers.

(b) Antagonists

The antagonists are muscles found on the opposite side of the joint to the muscles acting as prime movers.

(c) Fixators

Muscles act as fixators when they are working statically to fix part of the body in a stationary position whilst concentric or eccentric muscle work is going on in another part of the body.

Example: When a gardener is bent forward weeding, the hip and spine extensors are acting as fixators to keep the trunk bent forward in a static position while the arms move to pick the weeds.

From this, you can see that a muscle can be playing its part either as a prime mover or as an antagonist. For example, when a footballer kicks a ball forward, the hip flexors and the knee extensors are the prime movers.

The muscles on the opposite side of the knee and hip joint are the antagonists (that is, the hip extensors and knee flexors). When the footballer backheels the ball, the motion is reversed, and so are the terms for the muscles. The antagonists (which were the hip extensor and knee flexors) now become the prime movers and the prime movers for the forward kick now become the antagonists.

This is a lot to learn in a short space, but you will find it easier to remember if you think which muscles are doing what job as you practise your exercises. Try this exercise—it contains just about all the terms we have covered so far.

Feet astride, trunk forward at right angles to the legs. Arms stretched downwards from the shoulders. Raise the arms sideways and upwards to shoulder level—then lower back to the starting position. It is simple enough but a lot of muscles have been in action.

The extensors of the spine, hip and knee have been working *statically* as fixators to hold the position of the leg and trunk. When the arms are raised sideways and outwards, the extensors of the elbow work *statically* to keep them straight.

At the same time, the adductors and retractors of the arms and shoulder girdle (humerus and scapulae) work *concentrically* as *prime movers* to raise the arms. During this movement, the abductors of the arms and protractors of the shoulder blades (serratus anterior and pectorals) are the *antagonists*. When the arms are lowered under control, the same group of muscles responsible for raising the arms now work *eccentrically* to lower them under control to the starting position.

RANGE OF MOVEMENT

Most healthy joints have full range of movements. That is, they are able to move from full extension to full flexion (or from full abduction to full adduction), etc.

Diagram (a) shows the left arm from the side raising a weight from full extension of the elbow to full flexion.

This is known as full range of movement and is broken into three parts for analysis. Starting from full extension, the first third of the movement is known as the *outer range*, when the muscles are working at their longest length.

The next third is the *middle range* and it is within this range that the muscles are working to their best anatomical advantage. This is because a muscle pulls strongest when it is working approximately at right angles to the limb or bone it moves.

The final third is known as the *inner range*, when the muscles are working at their shortest length and closest to full flexion.

It would seem from this that the middle range is the most efficient

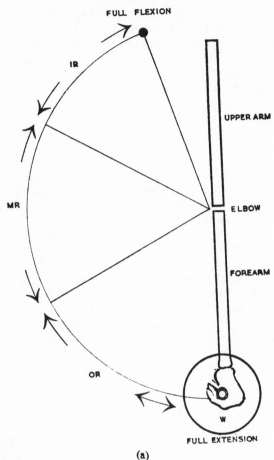

(a)

area anatomically for lifting weights, but this is outweighed by the mechanical disadvantage as the weight arm (that is, the length of lever from weight to fulcrum) has been increased. The reason is that when the weight reached the centre of the middle range (or when the forearm is horizontal) it is at its furthest point from the fulcrum, in this case the elbow. This factor makes the middle range the more difficult of the three for most movements.

The body, however, can be positioned in such a way that any of the three ranges may become the more difficult. As an example, in

Sit-ups, one of the other two ranges may become the most difficult. The exerciser lies on his back with hands clasped behind the head and feet secured on the ground. Keeping the trunk straight, the exerciser raises himself to a sitting position using the hip joints as the fulcrum and then continues the movement forwards towards the toes. In this case, the resistance is greatest as you start to raise the trunk and until you approach a position of forty-five degrees, hence in this case the outer range has proved the most difficult.

LEVERS

Leverage is broken down for study into the first class, the second class and the third class levers. We deal here only with the third class which is the most frequent in the body. Diagram (b) shows the third class lever. From the fulcrum to the point where power is applied, is known as the *power arm* and from the power to the weight is known as the *weight arm*.

When the weight is brought closer to the power, less effort is needed by the muscles which lift or hold it. The line of least resistance is generally when the weight is closest horizontally to that of the fulcrum. This is an important point to remember when the minimum of effort is needed to provide the maximum efficiency of movement.

From Diagram (b) you can see that in our bodies, the joints are the fulcrums, the bones are the levers and the power is supplied by the muscles.

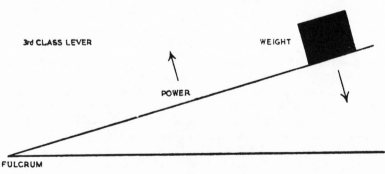

(b)

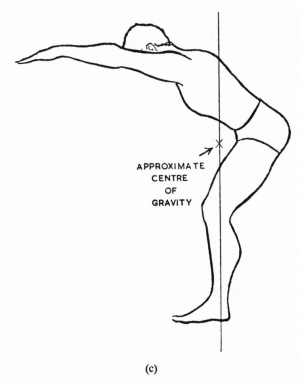

APPROXIMATE
CENTRE
OF
GRAVITY

(c)

BALANCE AND THE CENTRE OF GRAVITY

All objects have a centre of balance, known as the centre of gravity.
This is an imaginary spot in the centre of its weight.

In the human body, the centre of gravity is approximately halfway
between the soles of the feet and the crown of the head when standing. However, this is not a fixed point.

In Diagram (c) the dotted line is the vertical line passing through
the centre of gravity which shows that it can be outside the body. As
you lean the trunk forward from the hip joint, your centre of gravity
moves correspondingly further forward and downwards. Eventually
your centre of gravity will fall outside your base (that is, the feet)
and at this point you will overbalance forwards. Normally, of course,
your hips would move backwards to compensate for the forward and
downward movement of your trunk. When additional weight is being

handled by the body, the centre of gravity of the weight and body is now referred to as the *combined centre of gravity* and this falls somewhere between the centre of gravity of the body and the weight, the combined centre being nearer to whichever is the heavier.

THE PITFALLS OF ANALYSIS

So far we have dealt with the basics of kinesiology in what I hope has been a clear way. But to be fair to the new student of kinetics I should explain how easy it is to mistake the action of muscles in certain cases.

The analysis of movements performed on a vertical plane is relatively simple. The muscles which lift the object (whether it is a limb or a weight in the hand) are also responsible for lowering it under

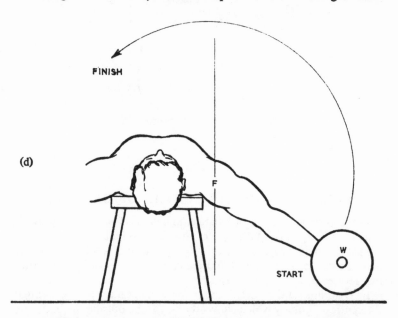

(d)

FINISH

F

START

W

control. The difficulty comes when the movement is a circular one in a vertical plane. Diagram (d) is an example of this. The athlete lies on his back on a form and is about to lift a dumb-bell off the ground with his right hand. If he lifts the weight from start to finish, he will have taken the weight through the full range of movement. As he raises the weight to the midway vertical line which runs through the

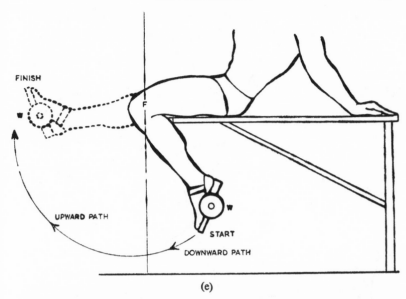

FINISH

UPWARD PATH

START

DOWNWARD PATH

(e)

fulcrum, he used the muscles on the front of his chest, shoulder and arms. Now once the weight passes the midline, it starts coming down. This means that its lowering must be controlled and the muscles on the opposite side of the shoulders and arms come into play. This is necessary as gravity is assisting in the downward movement of the weight after the midway line.

Diagram (e) is another example of how the muscles, when involved in handling weights, can change halfway through a smooth movement. The athlete is exercising by extending and flexing the knee with a legbell. At the start, the flexors (on the back of the thigh) will slowly lower the weight to the midline. As it begins the upward journey, the extensors of the knee which are on the other side of the joint will complete the movement. If the weight is removed and the movement is very fast, however, the knee extensors will be used from the starting position throughout the movement.

The importance of knowing which muscles are being used during various stages of an exercise is vital. It is sobering to think that there are still many sportsmen who are working through weight-training schedules that are of no particular help to their event. By learning which muscles are activating the movement, you need never fall into this error.

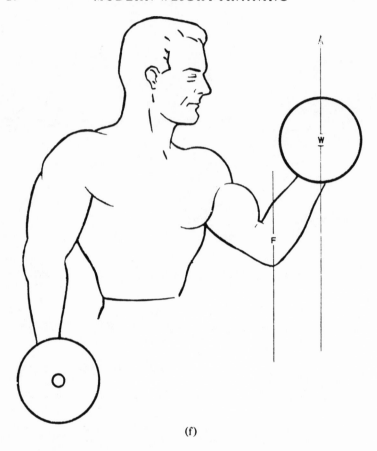

(f)

In view of this, a few more examples may prove of value to the keen student of the subject.

When wishing to obtain the greatest benefit in muscular development and strength, it is sometimes necessary to position the body so that the effective range of resistance can be increased at a given point.

In Diagram (f) we see an example of bad positioning of the arm for Curling. The weight line is approaching the fulcrum line and resistance is decreasing. Note the position of (F) elbow fulcrum in relation to (W) the weight. The weight arm is so short that little resistance is thrown on the flexors of the elbow. As soon as the weight

FINISH

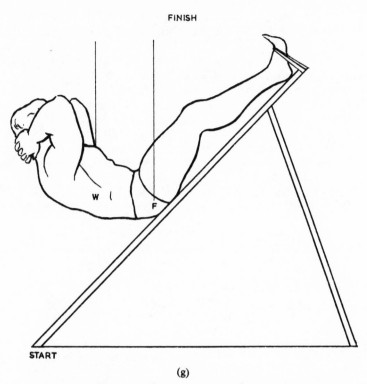

START

(g)

is vertically over the fulcrum no real effort is needed by the flexors. It is clear by the illustration that the movement in this position has little value in the inner range. For fast gains in muscular development, heavy inner range work is necessary.

EXCEPTIONS TO THE GENERAL RULE

We have already discussed sitting up from the back-lying position on the floor. Now let us consider the same movement, changed only by the angle at which it is performed. This is one of the few exceptions to the rule—as the vertical lines passing through the weight and fulcrum approach each other, resistance decreases. Diagram (g) shows how the body is positioned for this resistance to be thrown on the hip and spinal flexors in the middle and inner range. Note that in this case, even when the weight or trunk is vertically over the fulcrum (that is, the hip joint) the hip and spinal flexors are still working forcibly to hold the trunk in the vertical position. This is due to three things:

(*a*) The hamstrings at the back of the thigh are stretched and tend to pull the trunk backwards at this point.

(*b*) The abdomen is pressing on the thighs.

(*c*) The lack of mobility of the spine at this stage.

Other movements which are exceptions to the general principle involve one or all of the following factors:

(*a*) Elasticity of opposing muscle groups (antagonists).

(*b*) Soft tissue opposition (muscle or fat preventing two bones from coming together).

(*c*) Limitation of mobility at one or more joints.

To continue with similar types of movement which often lead to

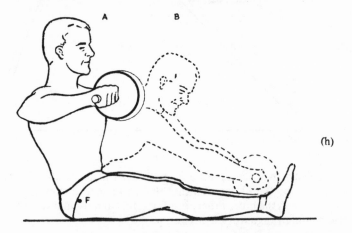

(h)

some confusion, Diagram (h) shows an exercise in which the head trunk and weight are brought towards the feet. It will be fairly easy to see that at position (A) at the start of the movement, slight resistance is thrown on the hip and spinal flexors, but as soon as the combined centre of gravity of trunk and weight moves past the vertical line passing through the fulcrum towards position (B), the hip and spinal extensors then begin to lower the trunk and weight eccentrically. Should the exerciser be very fat around the mid-section, with tight hamstrings, and should he perform the exercise *without weights*, then the flexors may work concentrically to overcome the

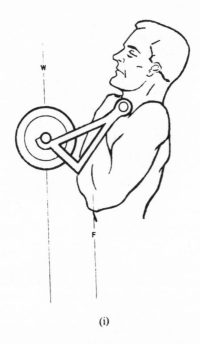

(i)

opposing resistance. That resistance is of course set up by the tight hamstrings and the fat tummy, which would come between the ribs and the thighs and restrict the forward movement.

To receive maximum resistance from a given weight at any one point throughout the full range of movement, the resistance must be applied at right angles to the moving limb or part of the body. If this theory is applied in practice to barbell or dumb-bell movements, it will be found that the moving limb will be at right angles to the pull of gravity when the greatest resistance is felt.

The other important factor is the angle at which the muscle pulls on a moving bone, remembering that a muscle is said to be working at its maximum efficiency when pulling at right angles to the moving bones. This is often misleading to the student of kinesiology. Take, for example, the simple movement of bringing a weight held in the hand from the side of the thigh to the shoulder in a half-circular movement (see page 21 containing full range of movement figure).

You will note that the resistance is at the greatest around the mid-point of full range, yet the muscles are pulling at right angles to the moving bones (forearm)—the most advantageous position anatomically. However, greater power is required to overcome a given resistance at this stage as the disadvantage of leverage (a longer weight arm) outweighs the anatomical advantage of the muscles pulling at right angles to the moving bones.

Diagram (i) shows the Peak Contraction Bell which is designed for this very purpose. You can see that as the flexion of the elbow is completed the weight does not act downwards in the same way as when a dumb-bell is held in the hand in the same position. You will notice there is a cross bar connecting the lower angle of the two triangular sides. This cross bar rests against the forearm nearly mid-way between the hand and the elbow. The downward pull of the weight at (W) tries to rotate at the cross bar resting against the mid-forearm and therefore the resistance of the weight is pulling the hand outwards and away from the shoulder at right angles to the forearm in the inner range.

MUSCLE PULL AT A POINT OF MECHANICAL DISADVANTAGE

A muscle or muscles are working at a great mechanical disadvantage when the line of muscle pull is at right angles to the gravitational pull, or when the line of muscle pull is at 180 degrees to the moving lever. See Diagram (j) showing Elbow Flexion.

When (W)—the weight— approaches the position vertically above the fulcrum (the elbow), the Weight Arm (W to F) rapidly diminishes. The muscle will then be pulling at its most advantageous position, that is, at right angles to the moving lever. Little or no effort is required by the elbow flexors at this stage.

Confusion can arise when one muscle works in two or more sections. Let us take the pectoralis major. It comes from the chest, crosses the front of the shoulder joint and is attached to the top front part of the humerus. But because it has two major attachments to the chest it has two main actions.

One section arises from the collar bone or clavicle, which is higher when standing than the end which is attached to the arm; therefore it pulls the arm inwards and upwards towards the midline of the chest. The second section is attached to the breast-bone or sternum which is lower than the attachment to the arm; therefore it pulls the

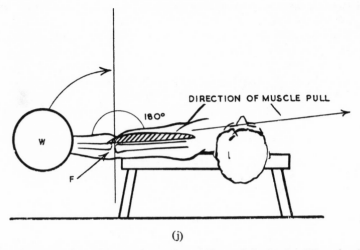

(j)

arm downwards and inwards to the midline of the body. When both sections are working, the movements are neutralized, and brought somewhere between the two extremes. (See 'Bent-arm Inclined Lateral Raise with Dumb-bells' in Chapter 13.)

The arms are being raised and lowered sideways whilst the trunk is at an angle. The upper fibres are working strongly to raise the arms to the overhead position. When the position of the body is reversed, with the head down and feet fixed at the high end of the bench and the exerciser performing the same movement (that is, arm raising and lowering sideways), the lower or sternal attachments of the pectorals are working strongly. (See 'Bent-arm Declined Lateral Raise with Dumb-bells' in Chaptei 13.)

An interesting fact is that two men may perforni the same move-ment with different results.

Take, for instance, two men performing this same exercise on a flat bench. 'A' has a very high and well-developed chest and 'B' has a very shallow flat chest. When back-lying, 'A's' sternum will be pointing forward and upwards and 'B's' sternum will be lying more or less parallel with the bench. In other words, 'A's' sternum is in the same position on a flat bench as 'B's' would be if he were lying on an incline bench at forty-five degrees with his feet fixed at the high end.

I have a colleague whose sternum, when lying on a flat bench, points almost vertically upwards. Therefore, when performing the

Lateral Raise with Two Dumb-bells, as described, his sternum and clavicle are almost in line with the vertical pathway of the arms.

Consequently, the complete pectoral is working whilst on a flat bench; the fibres are pulling in the direct line of action of the arms.

In this chapter I have given a few examples and comments which may assist you in your analysis. Principles of and important extracts from kinesiology have been re-emphasized.

CHAPTER 3

ANATOMY SIMPLIFIED

The study of anatomy, physiology and kinetics has always been very important to me. Even as a twelve-year-old boy, I was fascinated by books on anatomy and knew all the major bones and the names of many of the major muscles.

As I grew older my interest deepened and in my 'teens I had a very good knowledge of anatomy and physiology. This was extremely useful to me both as an active lifter and coach, and it gave me a flying start when I joined the Army Physical Training Corps in 1940.

Because of my interest in the body I applied for several remedial gymnastic courses during my army service. At the end of the War, I was one of the A.P.T.C. instructors who were selected for a post-war course in remedial gymnastics which took place at Pindersfield Hospital Training School and Leeds College of Anatomy.

During this period, I had the opportunity of listening to, and learning from many distinguished doctors and surgeons. I felt extremely sorry, however, for some of my colleagues who had not had a groundwork in anatomy and physiology similar to my own. I spent hours helping them by breaking down the lectures into simple language, so when I was appointed National Coach to the B.A.W.L.A. in 1948, with the training of instructors a major part of my job, I was able to present the subject of anatomy and kinetics in a more simple manner. In courses which lasted only two weekends we had wonderful success with the methods I shall describe in this chapter.

I am more convinced than ever that when teaching this subject in the early stages, the instructor must find the simplest way to present the basic principles.

Should you already know the major bones and features and have some knowledge of the origins, insertions and actions of the major muscles, then well and good. If on the other hand, you are a qualified teacher of physical education, or physiotherapist, this simplified chapter may assist you when teaching others.

I use the principles of association by connecting lay terms with the medical names for the major bones, such as the lay term shin-bone (tibia), shoulder-blade (scapula), collar-bone (clavicle) and so on.

All you need to know about the skeleton, beginning from the foot, is as follows:

Heel-bone   Calcaneus
Shin-bone   Tibia
(The thin bone which lies parallel to the shin and on the outside of
  the lower leg has no lay term and is known as the fibula.)
Knee-cap   Patella
Thigh-bone   Femur
Pelvis   (The term 'pelvis' we can use as it is fairly
                     widely understood. This is the bowl-shaped
                     bone which in a way acts as base or floor for
                     the abdominal organs.)
Backbone   Spine (which is based from the sacrum at the
                     mid rear of the pelvis, and extends to the
                     skull. It is made up of small bones called
                     vertebrae and is divided into three main
                     sections:

                       (I) The neck (or cervical region)
                       (II) The chest (or thoracic region)
                       (III) The waist (or lumbar region)
                     The joints between these many bones permit
                     one to turn, twist and bend in most directions.
Chest or rib box   Thorax
Shoulder-blade   Scapula
Collar-bone   Clavicle
Breast-bone   Sternum
Upper arm bone   Humerus
Forearm bone   (The forearm bones have no lay terms. When
                     one turns the palms to the front in the stand-
                     ing position, the two forearm bones lie parallel
                     from the elbow to the hand. The bone on the
                     thumb side of the forearm is the radius, the
                     other bone on the little finger side is known
                     as the ulna.)

As this is a chapter covering the simple and basic factors of
anatomy, many small bones such as those of the hand and foot are
omitted. So also are many other important anatomical features,
which should be studied at a later date if the reader's interest develops.

The actual names of muscles are omitted at this stage because here
we deal with muscle groups and their actions as such.

The chart at the end of this chapter is simple to follow and makes
clear the actions permitted at each joint, and the muscle group which

activates these joints. The medical terms for the actions permitted at each joint are not difficult:

Flexion	Bending	⎧ These two movements are the
Extension	Straightening	⎨ most common and are possible at all major joints.

Adduction   To bring towards the mid-line of the body as in bringing the shoulder blades together.

Abduction   To take apart, or away from the mid-line of the body, as in jumping astride. The opposite of adduction.

Circumduction   To circle part of the body from a point, such as arms circling from the point of the shoulder joint.

Rotation   To turn outwards and inwards without changing the position of the long axis of the bone or bones as in turning the head from left to right. This is rotation of the cervical region.

Elevation   To raise—as in raising the shoulders when shrugging.

Depression   To pull downwards—as in pulling the shoulders downwards.

(Elevation and depression apply to movement of the shoulder girdle, scapula and clavicle.)

Hyper-extension To extend beyond the normal—as in arching the back in the back-lying position.

Once you are familiar with the actions permitted at each joint, it is easy to learn the names of the muscle groups which produce the movement. Take, for example, the knee-joint. Extension of the knee is produced by the extensors, flexion by the flexors and so on.

This chart is laid out in six columns as follows:

Column 1.   Shows the movement permitted at each joint.

  ,,   2.   Shows the muscle group which produces the joint action.

  ,,   3.   Gives the name of the major muscles employed in the group action.

  ,,   4.   Indicates the position of the muscle group.

  ,,   5.   Gives the position at which the muscle group tendons cross the acting joint.

  ,,   6.   Gives a list of activities which employ the muscle groups.

With the information found in this chapter, you will be in a position to analyse most major sport and athletic movements.

Undoubtedly a deeper knowledge of anatomy and kinesiology is of great advantage to the reader who wishes to improve his status as a coach. I would advise him to obtain a copy of *The Principles of Anatomy and Physiology for P.T. Instructors*, published by H.M.S.O.

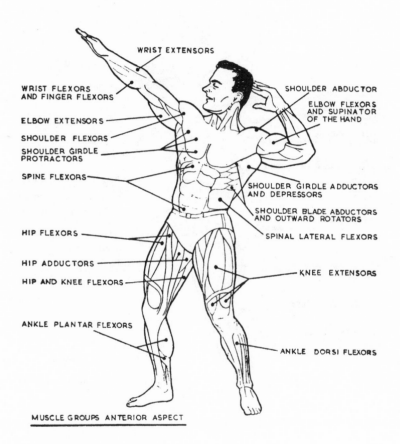

WRIST EXTENSORS

WRIST FLEXORS
AND FINGER FLEXORS

ELBOW EXTENSORS

SHOULDER FLEXORS

SHOULDER GIRDLE
PROTRACTORS

SPINE FLEXORS

HIP FLEXORS

HIP ADDUCTORS

HIP AND KNEE FLEXORS

ANKLE PLANTAR FLEXORS

SHOULDER ABDUCTOR

ELBOW FLEXORS
AND SUPINATOR
OF THE HAND

SHOULDER GIRDLE ADDUCTORS
AND DEPRESSORS

SHOULDER BLADE ABDUCTORS
AND OUTWARD ROTATORS

SPINAL LATERAL FLEXORS

KNEE EXTENSORS

ANKLE DORSI FLEXORS

MUSCLE GROUPS ANTERIOR ASPECT

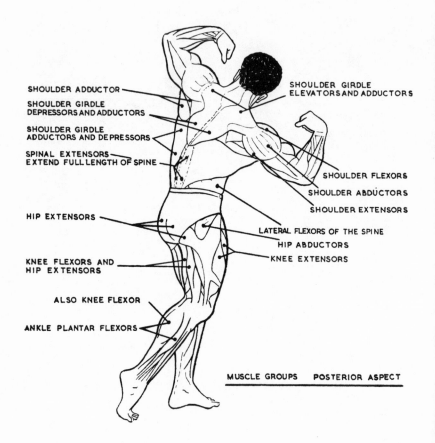

SHOULDER ADDUCTOR

SHOULDER GIRDLE
DEPRESSORS AND ADDUCTORS

SHOULDER GIRDLE
ADDUCTORS AND DEPRESSORS

SPINAL EXTENSORS
EXTEND FULL LENGTH OF SPINE

HIP EXTENSORS

KNEE FLEXORS AND
HIP EXTENSORS

ALSO KNEE FLEXOR

ANKLE PLANTAR FLEXORS

SHOULDER GIRDLE
ELEVATORS AND ADDUCTORS

SHOULDER FLEXORS

SHOULDER ABDUCTORS

SHOULDER EXTENSORS

LATERAL FLEXORS OF THE SPINE

HIP ABDUCTORS

KNEE EXTENSORS

MUSCLE GROUPS   POSTERIOR ASPECT

1. Joint Action	2. Muscle Group and Action	3. Major Muscles	4. Muscle Group Position	5. Position of Acting Tendon	6. Exercises & Sports Involving These Muscles & Joints.
ANKLE Planter Flexion	Planter Flexors raise the heel and point the toe away from knee	Gastrocnemius soleus	Back of lower leg	Crosses back of ankle joint. Attached to rear of heel	Heel raising of any description. All forms of running and jumping, walking and dancing.
ANKLE Dorsi-flexion	Dorsi-flexors. Raise the toes and foot towards knee	Tibialis anticus	Front outside of lower leg	Crosses diagonally inwards the front of ankle joint. Attached near root of great toe	Although the action is to pull the back of the foot towards the front of the shin, you will find the planter flexors work in conjunction with the planter flexors above, during certain movements.
KNEE Flexion	Flexors—bend the knee. Pull heel towards hip. Also accessory extensors of the hip. See hip extension	*Hamstring Group* Bicep femoris Semi tendinous ,, membranous (Gastrocnemius: see ankle)	Back of thigh	Crosses back and sides of knee joint. Attached near front, top part, of lower leg	Used in all movements where the knee is bent as in kicking backwards with the heel, but these muscles greatly assist in hip extension used in walking, running, jumping and lifting weights from the floor.
KNEE Extension	Extensors, straighten knee in kicking movement	*Quadriceps Group* Vastus internus ,, externus ,, medialis Rectus femoris	Front of thigh	Crosses front of knee joint. Attached lower leg just below knee joint	Used in forward kicking, running, jumping, walking, dancing, swimming and rock climbing, lifting.
HIP Flexion	Flexors—bring thigh forwards and upwards towards chest	Iliopsoas Rectus femoris } Sartorius	Front of spine and pelvis, internally. Front top inside of thigh	Crosses front of hip joint. Attachments above and below hip joint	Used in all movement bringing the thigh forwards and upwards when running, jumping, walking, dancing and swimming. Whilst back lying trunk fixed raises legs upwards. When feet fixed raises trunk to sitting position.

1. JOINT ACTION	2. MUSCLE GROUP AND ACTION	3. MAJOR MUSCLES	4. MUSCLE GROUP POSITION	5. POSITION OF ACTING TENDON	6. EXERCISES & SPORTS INVOLVING THESE MUSCLES & JOINTS.
HIP Extension	Extensors, bring thigh backwards as in walking backwards, also raises the trunk when bent forward	*Hamstring Group* (*see* knee flexion) Gluteus maximus	Rear of hip and pelvis, back of thigh. (*see knee* flexion)	Crosses back aspect of hip joint. Attachments rear, top of thigh. Also back of thigh (*see* knee flexion)	Used a great deal in lifting from the floor, jumping, rock climbing. Kicking backwards as in some swimming movements. Running, walking, etc.
HIP Adduction	Adductors—bring the thighs together from the feet-astride position	Adductor longus ,, brevis ,, magnus	Inside and back of thigh	Comes from the pelvis between the legs, crosses the inside hip joint and is attached to the back of the thigh bone	Used in all forms of jumping especially where the knees are turned outwards when the legs are bent prior to leaping upwards. Used in swimming, horse riding and in conjunction with other hip and leg movements.
HIP Abduction	Abductors, pull the leg sideways from the feet-together position	Gluteus minimus ,, medius	Lies on the side and rear of hip	Crosses the outside of the hip joint	Used in feet-astride jumping in gymnastics, breast stroke swimming and is active in many hip and leg movements.
HIP ROTATION Inwards Outwards	Inwards rotators rotate the thigh bone inwards within its own axis Outward rotators rotate the thigh bone outwards within its own axis	The muscles which flex, extend, abduct and adduct the thigh to the hip bone also act to assist in the rotation inwards and outwards			Used in almost every leg and hip movement.
SPINE Flexion	Flexors, round or bend the spine forwards as in raising the head and shoulders only from the lying position	*Abdominals* Rectus abdominis Transversus ,, Internal and external obliques	Form the front and side walls of the abdomen	Muscles and tendons cross the gap in front of the body from the lower ribs to the front of the pelvis	Used in sitting up from the lying position twisting the trunk from side to side when lying or standing. Used in forward throwing and in any movements where the spine is forcibly bent against resistance.

1. Joint Action	2. Muscle Group and Action	3. Major Muscles	4. Muscle Group Position	5. Position of Acting Tendon	6. Exercises & Sports Involving These Muscles & Joints.
SPINE Extension	Extensors—extend or straighten the opposite direction from flexion (hyperextension) where extension passes the vertical or straight line, as in back arching	Extensors of spine —a collection of small muscles grouped together and too numerous to list	These are two columns of muscles which run on either side of the spine and extend from the pelvis at the rear all the way to the skull	These muscles and tendons are attached to the pelvis, ribs, spine and skull	Back arching or bending backwards while lying face down. Used vigorously in all forms of lifting and when coming from the bent forward position to standing position. When one column is the major one acting them they produce side bending or bring the body from a side-bent position to the erect position. They also assist in other movements.
SPINE Lateral Flexion Spinal Rotation	See Flexors and Extensors of Spine Lateral flexion and rotation of the spine are produced by the spinal extensors and flexors working in various combinations				Used in almost every sport that involves turning, bending or straightening of the trunk. e.g. golf, tennis, discus throwing, polo etc. etc.

1. Joint Action	2. Muscle Group and Action	3. Major Muscles	4. Muscle Group Position	5. Position of Acting Tendon	6. Exercises & Sports Involving These Muscles & Joints.
SHOULDER Elevation	Elevators—raise the shoulder girdle, which includes the arm, scapula (shoulder blade) and clavicle (collar bone)	Trapezius Levator scapulae Assisted by: rhomboids	On the back of the neck and above the scapula	The muscles are attached to the scapula and when this is raised the arm and clavicle are raised also, as these are attached to the scapula	Used in almost all movements involving arm action.
SHOULDER Depression	Depressors—pull the shoulder girdle downwards	Latissimus dorsi Lower trapezius Part of pectorals	Lower back and lower chest	Latissimus dorsi and pectoralis major attached to the front, top part of the upper arm bone (humerus)	Used in movements where downward pressure is applied by the arms as in rope climbing, certain strokes in racquet games, gymnastics, etc.
SHOULDER JOINT Flexion	Flexors—raise the arms forwards and upwards	Anterior deltoids Serratus anterior Trapezius	Front of shoulder side and rear of chest	Deltoid crosses front of shoulder joint. Other muscles rotate the scapula outwards	Used in all exercises and movements which require forward and upward action of the arm. Underarm bowling, etc. All overhead weight lifting movements.
SHOULDER JOINT Extension	Extensors—pull the arm backwards and upwards (opposite to flexion)	Posterior deltoids Long head of tricep	Back of shoulder joint	Crosses back of shoulder joint	All movements where the elbow or arm is raised backwards, e.g. rope and rock climbing, chinning the bar.
SHOULDER JOINT Abduction	Abductors—raise the arm sideways	Deltoids Serratus anterior Trapezius	Deltoids: front, side and rear of shoulder joint, serratus and trapezius, side and back of chest	Deltoids cross side, front and rear of shoulder joint. Other muscles rotate the scapula outwards	All movements where the arm is raised sideways away from the body against resistance e.g. pulling weights from the floor to the chest. Most movements involving upward arm and shoulder action.

1. JOINT ACTION	2. MUSCLE GROUP AND ACTION	3. MAJOR MUSCLES	4. MUSCLE GROUP POSITION	5. POSITION OF ACTING TENDON	6. EXERCISES & SPORTS INVOLVING THESE MUSCLES & JOINTS.
SHOULDER JOINT Adduction	Adductors—pull the arm in towards the side of the body	Teres major and minor. Pectorals. Latissimus dorsi	The front and back of the chest	Crosses between body and arm	Rope and mountain climbing or any downward movements of the arms against resistance
SHOULDER JOINT Circumduction		Involves co-ordination of shoulder flexors, extensors, abductors and adductors			
ELBOW Flexion	Flexors—bend the arm to bring the hand toward the shoulders	Brachialis anticus Bicep	Lies on front of upper arm	Crosses front of elbow joint. (Also crosses front of shoulder joint)	All arm flexing movements against resistance, e.g. rope and mountain climbing.
ELBOW Extension	Extensors—straighten the arm against resistance	Tricep	Back of upper arm	Crosses back of elbow joint	All movements where the elbow is straightened against resistance such as shot putt, punching, certain strokes in racquet games; all forms of overhead lifting, etc.
WRIST Flexion	Flexors—bend the palm of the hand upwards towards the forearm	These are too numerous to list	Lie on the front of the fore-arm when the palm is facing forwards	Cross the front of the wrist	Used in all gripping movements or forward wrist movements.
WRIST Extension	Extensors—pull the back of the hand towards the back of the arm	Too numerous to list	Back of forearm	Cross the back of the wrist	Used in all forms of gripping or movements requiring wrist action.

N.B. This chart has been kept as simple as possible. Many muscles which assist most movements described have been omitted purposely to keep the names of the muscles down to a minimum. Many actions are a combination of muscular movements and are not as pure as this chart may indicate. The positions of the muscles and where they cross the joint or joints are approximate but are sufficient to enable the student at this stage to have a fairly good idea how to analyse major movements. For the student who wishes to take the next stage in study, I would like to recommend the R.A.F. book, *The Principles of Anatomy and Physiology for Physical Training Instructors.*

CHAPTER 4

BREATHING

A lot of conflicting advice has been given about breathing during weight-training. Much of this isn't based on any scientific reasoning so I would like to make some observations on the subject which are physiologically correct.

With a few exceptions, it is advisable to breathe in on the effort. That is, you should breathe in as you lift the weight and out as you lower it.

Let me give examples of how important the right form of breathing can be.

For the Full Squat with the weight across the shoulders, it is generally advised to fill the lungs with air, then go down and up and then breathe out as you return to the upright position. In theory, for chest expansion, this is right, for as you reach the bottom position the abdominal organs are forced up against the diaphragm which pushes upwards against the lungs which in turn force the ribs out sideways and extend the thorax. This is the purpose of the exercise, so the theory is quite sound.

It is sometimes suggested that the breath should be held while two or even three squats are performed. It is believed, though, that by doing this over a number of years, you could distend the alveoli of the lungs which may cause lung complaints in later life. To my knowledge there is no medical evidence to support this. I would, however, recommend that the individual breathes out as he reaches the bottom position of the Full Squat and then fills his lungs on the effort of rising.

Now for the Bench Press. In this, the individual will lie on his back on a narrow bench, then press the barbell from a resting position on his chest to arms' length finishing with the barbell vertically over the shoulder joints.

Many people recommend that you should breathe out as you press the weight upwards. I can only mention that I broke the British record several times with a similar movement by doing just the opposite—breathing in as I pressed.

So let's break down this movement and see what we find. The weight is raised by the muscles on the front of the chest and shoulders, assisted by those which bring the shoulder-blades away from the spine and the muscles which extend the arms. All these muscles are attached either directly or indirectly to the thorax. Therefore, if you pack the lungs with air by breathing in as you start the movement, then the muscles which raise the arms will have a fixed, solid base from which to work.

By breathing out during this exercise, the muscles have a less-solid base from which to work.

These are only two examples in which teaching on breathing is incorrect; there are others. But you can work out your own method of breathing for a particular exercise or lift once you have grasped the basic facts about anatomy.

For example, when the exerciser tends to round the spine, the ribs will then be depressed, the size of the thorax reduced and therefore an indication that one should breathe out.

When the exercise produces extension of the spine, the ribs are elevated and breathing in is therefore indicated.

The first case is evident in abdominal exercises where the trunk is brought from the back-lying position into a sitting position by flexing the spine and hips. The effort is made on the upward part of the movement, but according to what we've already seen, the exerciser should breathe *out* as the spine is flexed on the effort and *in* when returning to the back-lying position.

The breathing discussed refers to movements performed during normal weight training and consisting of eight, ten or more repetitions and not to *record* or *limit* attempts when the breathing may differ from that laid down for a general guide.

CHAPTER 5

WEIGHT-TRAINING TERMS

The Single Set System

Or *Simple System* when the exerciser or coach decides that one set or group of repetitions should be enough on each exercise. The number of repetitions on this set depends on the fitness, experience and objective of the exerciser, and can vary from a few repetitions to as high as fifty where endurance is the objective.

Multiple Sets System

The exerciser repeats the same exercise in sets or groups of repetitions. The popular number is three or four sets of eight repetitions. This permits the exerciser to perform twenty-four repetitions with heavier resistance than is possible when twenty-four repetitions are carried out in one set without a rest. The heavier resistance provides better results in strength and development. Some body builders, for development, use as much as ten sets of ten repetitions. Louis Martin, our great World Middle-heavyweight Champion has used ten sets of two. The latter permits the use of very heavy weights and can produce real power.

Strict Technique

The exerciser adheres to good body positions and when the aim is to develop the arm muscles, the exerciser does not permit the back or legs to assist the movement. Usually the basic starting position is not changed during the movement made by the part of the body being exercised.

Cheating Technique

This is the opposite of the Strict Technique. Here, the individual will use accessory muscles other than those actually necessary to produce the movement, to assist in the first two ranges of movement, finishing in a strict position in the inner range with the normal group of muscles. In this way, greater resistance can be applied in the inner range.

Example: When performing the Two Hands Curl in Strict Technique the body is erect and the barbell is held at arms' length, palms to the front and resting against the thighs. The arms are bent and the barbell comes up to the top of the chest. Principally, the flexors of the elbow have been used, so this is Strict Technique. In this exercise, the greatest resistance is felt in the middle range. By the *Cheating Technique* heavier weights can be used. In the Two Hands Curl, instead of standing erect, the knees are slightly bent and the body leans forwards a little. At the start of the movement the legs and body are straightened quickly. At the same time, the elbows bend to lift the weight to the chest. The momentum gained in straightening the legs and back will help you to carry a heavier weight through the middle range (in this exercise, the most difficult) and leave you to finish the inner range (final third) of the Curl in the Strict Technique, yet with resistance far greater than that used in the strict version.

Specific Movement

Where movement is isolated to exercise a small group of muscles in Strict Technique, or when the body is positioned to throw the greatest resistance in a particular range.

Massive Movements

This is the reverse of specific exercise. Here you are co-ordinating large groups of muscles which enables you to handle greater resistance and in turn demands are made on the cardio-vascular systems. Power and ruggedness are developed.

Peak Contraction Exercises

These are similar to Specific Movement exercises except that you position your body so that when you finish the movement you will get the greatest load not in the middle range as is normal, but in the inner range. The muscle or muscles will then be working hardest when operating at their shortest length.

Flushing

One group of muscles are bombarded with one set of repetitions after another. The term comes from the belief that in doing this, the muscle is flushed with blood. This is a fast way of developing a particular muscle, and as a word of warning, it is not wise to attempt flushing on more than one or two groups of muscles within the same schedule, as the demand on time and energy may be too great.

Alternate Set Systems

Though you still attack the same part of the body with the alternate sets system, you don't attack the same group of muscles. Should you be concentrating on your upper arm, you might alternate your sets with an elbow extension exercise and elbow flexion exercise, continuing for the required number of sets.

The Time-Plus-Poundage System

Instead of performing an exercise with a specific poundage and repetitions at the normal speed, an attempt is made to reduce the time taken to perform the exercise by speeding up the movement and reducing the rest pause between sets. This method has been found effective in the development of muscle bulk and fitness but when light weight and high repetitions are used, little gains are to be found in power. Experience has also shown that this type of development is not of a lasting nature.

Continuous Exercise System

The purpose of this system is to exercise different muscle groups, so permitting the exerciser to move quickly from one exercise to another, thereby keeping the pulse rate high and providing exercise for the heart and lungs as well as the muscles and joints. This is not feasible to the same degree with the set system, where the same muscle group is exercised in sets of repetitions e.g. 8–8–8–8; the rest pauses between each set of 8 are necessary to recover from local fatigue, these permit the pulse rate to drop, and the value of heart and lung power is diminished. For all round fitness and physical efficiency of a general nature, the rests must be cut down, and eventually eliminated. The aim should be to perform the greatest volume of work in the shortest period of time.

CHAPTER 6

SCHEDULE CONSTRUCTION

It may sound obvious but one of the most important things to be decided before you work out a schedule is to know exactly what you want to accomplish with it.

Let's take an example by working out a schedule for an absolute beginner who has never lifted weights before. We'll assume that his objective is a reasonable standard of fitness and development. We can break him in gently by providing:

(a) *Mobility.* To stretch his muscles over ranges they may never have covered before.

(b) *Balance and Control.* To get him accustomed to the balance needed for handling weights.

To learn this balance and control without actually testing the body with heavy weights, the beginner should go through his schedule using an empty bar which weighs approximately 15 lb.

Now for the schedule. It should contain at least one movement for each of the major parts of the body but tackled in a physiological sequence. This sequence should follow the pattern of mild exercises at first, the intensity of the work increasing as the body warms up. The schedule can then finish with exercises which do not demand a great deal from the cardio-vascular systems.

Our beginner should start with warming-up free standing exercises for three or four minutes, such as running on the spot, or feet astride jumping with arms raising sideways, trunk turning and so on. Then comes the warming up with weights. This exercise should involve the major group of muscles of the arms, trunk and legs. The exerciser can next move on to an exercise for the arms and shoulders, followed by an upper back exercise. He concludes this position with a trunk exercise, and probably another arm exercise.

By now, our beginner should be warm enough to perform a massive movement such as the Full Squat.

He follows with an exercise that will allow the large leg and back muscles to relax—a back-lying exercise such as the Bench Press or Bent Arm Lateral Raise. The body will now be ready for another massive movement; so try the Power Clean in which the insteps are placed beneath the bar, gripping the barbell shoulder-width apart with the hands, keeping the knuckles to the front, the knees bent and the back flat. The barbell should be pulled vigorously from the floor to rest on the chest. This will soon get the beginner breathing heavily, so he should follow up with another leg-resting exercise such as the Bent Arm Pullover while lying on a bench.

Finally, our beginner can conclude his simple schedule with a calf exercise and an abdominal exercise.

A newcomer to weight training should not plan his schedule to produce muscles overnight. One set, each of ten to twelve repetitions, on each movement, is enough to get the person accustomed to the balance and control of weights, to mobilize his joints and get him reasonably fit. The weights or discs can be added after two training periods with the empty bar.

This schedule can be retained by the beginner for the first two or three weeks assuming he has training sessions three times a week.

Now the individual can move from the beginner's to the intermediate stage in which the set system is adopted. Here, he will perform two sets of each movement during his schedule instead of one at the beginning of his training, with a rest pause between each. Assuming the amount of training continues (and the three sessions a week should preferably be held on alternate days) he will pass out of the intermediate stage in another two weeks.

From here, the individual will move on to what is known as the normal body-building stage in which he will perform three or four sets of seven or eight repetitions on each movement. Advanced body-building follows. This is made up of a mixture of three to four sets of most movements and five to eight sets of specific movements in which the exerciser hopes to specialize.

From here onwards, time will play a big factor and *if* the individual can train six times a week, then he can go on to arm and chest exercises on Monday, Wednesdays and Fridays, leg and back exercises on Tuesdays, Thursdays and Saturdays. I've shown here that the purpose in mind was to progress from a simple keep-fit schedule through intermediate stages of body-building, right on to advanced body-building.

Now I neither condemn nor condone the extreme stages of body-building, but I think most coaches, and weight-training advisers, would feel that if the end product of all this was *only* a magnificent physique, then it could be a waste of time.

Training six nights a week to produce just a prize-winning physique may seem vain, even abnormal, but I would not argue against it for there are a thousand other things the individual could do which would be much worse for his health or character.

Finally on this point I'd like to add that I feel physical training should have far more meaning than the improvement of one's physique alone. Efficiency in fitness, strength, speed, endurance and skill is far more important.

The fact that such world-champion lifters as Tommy Kono and Louis Martin have also prize-winning physiques is more by coincidence than design. These are physiques proved to be functional and therefore earn greater respect.

I. TYPICAL SCHEDULE FOR BEGINNER

(*Poundage*. Select a weight which permits the correct execution of the exercise and repetitions laid down.)

		Repetitions
Exercise		*Set 1*
1. High Pull-ups to Forehead	. .	9 working up to 12
2. Press behind Neck	. . .	9 ,, ,, ,, 12
3. Curl	.	9 ,, ,, ,, 12
4. Side Bend with One Dumb-bell	.	9 ,, ,, ,, 12
5. Bent-forward Rowing	. . .	9 ,, ,, ,, 12
6. Squat, Bar behind Neck	. .	10 ,, ,, ,, 15
7. Bench Press, normal grip	. .	10 ,, ,, ,, 15
8. Clean to Chest	. . .	6 ,, ,, ,, 10
9. Pull-over (Breathing)	. .	8 ,, ,, ,, 14
10. Sit-ups without weights	. .	6 ,, ,, ,, 14

II. TYPICAL SCHEDULE OF INTERMEDIATE STAGE

(*Poundage*. Select a weight which permits the correct execution of the exercise and repetitions laid down.)

	Repetitions	
Exercise	*Set 1*	*Set 2*
1. High Pull-ups from Knees to Arms' Length Overhead	10	—
2. Press behind Neck	8	8
3. Curl	8	8
4. Side Bend with One Dumb-bell . .	10	8
5. Bent-forward Rowing	8	8
6. Squat, Bar behind Neck . . .	10	8

		Repetitions	
		Set 1	Set 2
7. Bench Press		10	8
8. Clean to Chest		6	6
9. Bent-arm Pull-over		8	8
10. Sit-ups without weights		10	10

III. TYPICAL SCHEDULE OF ADVANCED STAGE

(*Poundage*. Select a weight which permits the correct execution of the exercise and repetitions laid down.)

Exercise	Set 1	Repetitions Set 2	Set 3	Set 4
1. Power Clean to Chest .	5	5	5	—
2. Seated Press from Chest .	7	7	6	5
3. Dumb-bell Screw Curl .	8	8	8	—
4. Shot Side Bend . .	10	10	(each side)	
5. Bent-forward Single-arm Rowing . . .	7	7	7 (each side)	
6. Front Squat . . .	10	(Poundage in this exercise		
	8	to be increased by 10 lb.		
	6	as repetitions decrease.		
	4	Limit poundage with		
		4 reps.)		
7. Bench Press with Two Dumb-bells . . .	10	8	7	7
8. Clean to Chest with Two Dumb-bells . . .	5	5	5	5
9. Bent-arm Pull-over with Centrally-loaded Dumb-bell	10	9	8	—
10. Abdominal Exercise . (Select one from list in this book.)	10	10	10	—

You will note that some of the exercises contain relatively more work than others.

This conforms with the principle I have discussed whereby it is neither necessary nor advisable to perform more than three sets on *all exercises.*

More than three sets should only be applied to specific parts of the body selected for specialization.

CHAPTER 7

VARIATION OF SCHEDULES TO ALTER RESULTS

Although training with weights is usually associated with strength and power, by varying the repetitions, sets, speed of movement and the rest pause between exercises and sets, one can produce fitness, power, endurance or speed. These I will deal with more fully in a later chapter, here stating the principles and broadly how they can be followed.

FITNESS

I feel certain that fitness training with weights has not been fully exploited simply because the coach or athlete often allows the basic conception of power-building to drag him from his first objective—fitness.

Despite the fact that the weight should be kept light for general fitness, the exercises need not become as boring as free standing movements, for the exerciser will be able to judge his progress by the manner in which he handles a given poundage or by increasing the poundage or repetition as his general fitness improves.

When training for fitness, there are three important points to bear in mind: (a) Type of exercise. (b) Repetitions and Sets. (c) Rest pause.

(a) *Type of Exercise.* The type needed for general fitness are those which will activate collective groups of muscles and would not include specialized individual muscle exercises which might employ only one joint action, as no great demand would be placed on the cardio-vascular system (heart and lungs). It *is* this demand that is so necessary for fitness. The correct type of exercises for fitness are the High Pull-ups, the Standing Cleans, Alternate One-hand Swinging, Squats of all forms and most types of cheating exercises which co-ordinate the larger muscle groups.

(b) *Repetitions.* One can select 5 to 8 of the above exercises. The repetitions should not be less than 10 to begin with. This ensures that the weight will provide moderate resistance. When that number is achieved in comfort, it can be increased in easy stages to 20 or even 30. When the chosen maximum is reached, the weight which previously allowed 10 repetitions is increased and one works up to a maximum as before. The resistance selection is almost automatic. If 10 is the maximum repetition, then a weight must be selected that can be used for that number while still performing the exercise in the correct manner with ease.

(c) *The Rest Pause*. This will depend on your present state of fitness and ambitions. Generally, one would wait just long enough between sets or exercises for breathing to return *almost* to normal. This would vary from about 1½ minutes to just over 2 minutes, again depending on the number of repetitions and the resistance used. At first, the exerciser should time these rest pauses and then make an effort to cut them down as he improves in fitness. The higher repetitions throw a healthy demand on the cardio-vascular system. This means that the exerciser will be breathing forcibly after, say, 18 repetitions with resistance that just permits that number. This type of programme is advisable for the beginner who finds himself in a state of physical condition below par. The degree of fitness to be attained will depend on the requirements of the individual, the times available for training and his or her enthusiasm.

Let us look at two extremes. First of all, a businessman whose only wish is to reach a fairly good standard of fitness for his age; and secondly, the young man who leads an active life in various sports.

The businessman will simply follow the suggestions laid down in the first part of Chapter 1. The young man, on the other hand, will step up the speed of his movements, cut down on the rest pauses, increase the number of his repetitions and repeat some of the exercises already being performed so that he is doing two or more sets of repetition for some of the exercises.

The young man may then even introduce one or two severe exercises such as upward leaping with the barbell held behind the neck. It is quite possible that after a few months, by using heavier weights, and increasing the repetitions and sets than used at first, he will actually have been able to cut down the total time of his training period. By the mere fact that his improved fitness will have given him an improved rate of recovery, he will be able to cut down on the rest pause between exercises and sets.

ENDURANCE

This is just an extension to the advanced fitness aimed at by the young man above. The repetition can be increased from 20 to as much as 50. Naturally enough, the number of exercises attempted at one exercise period will drop, it might be two or four massive exercises (those co-ordinating movements using several joints and large groups of muscles). Again the theme is light resistance, high repetition, fast movements and short rest pauses (finally eliminated).

STRENGTH AND POWER

The development of strength and power requires almost the opposite procedure from endurance as far as resistance and repetitions are concerned. The weight used should not permit more than 5 repetitions and the total number of repetitions and sets should not exceed 20 to 25.

In some cases, the repetitions can total as little as 5 single attempts. As an example, the dead lift (merely lifting a weight from the floor to the thighs by straightening the legs and back) may fall somewhere in the last half of your power programme.

You will naturally be warmed up by then and find that you can proceed as follows:

```
1 repetition with 300 lb.
1     ,,        ,,  325 ,,
1     ,,        ,,  345 ,,
1     ,,        ,,  360 ,,
1     ,,        ,,  370 ,,
```

The last repetition would be near enough your training limit on this movement. It has a leaning towards a pure strength movement as it requires little speed or technique, but we will deal with this later.

SPEED

Speed is a quality whereby the muscle acts against a given resistance, producing fast movement at a joint or joints far beyond the normal action. There is a very fine dividing line between the power and speed, between the Olympic lifter and the speed and power of the sprinter.

The Olympic lifter requires a higher degree of strength in his power as the resistance he must overcome is far greater than that of the sprinter. The resistance, being greater, reduces the speed of the movement. Nevertheless, the mental drive of the lifter is every bit as great as that of the sprinter. He must get the weight moving fast.

One talks of speed, and of an athlete being the fastest in the world, but this can often be incorrect. To say that a man is fast because he covers many miles in a record time is extremely misleading as this is principally endurance. But when a man is fast over a very short distance, or in performing a single action like punching, kicking, leaping, springing or turning, then this to me is speed.

The muscles must possess the strength to activate the joints against resistance set up by the body, part of the body or some outside resistance in the shortest possible time.

A combination of pure strength work, power work, and light fast movement with weights, correctly blended with the athlete's own event will greatly improve his speed.

CHAPTER 8

THE PRINCIPLES OF BODY MECHANICS AND ATHLETICS

My work with Geoff Dyson (who was at the time chief coach of the Amateur Athletic Association) prompted me to divide weight-training for athletics into three distinct phases for purposes of analysis.

General Weight-training

Irrespective of the sport or the event, it is always advisable to spend a few weeks and in some cases even months on a basic weight training schedule.

This builds general all-round power and gives the athlete the feel and balance required to handle weights.

Specific Weight-training

Here we require a good knowledge of the physical action of the event, for which we are about to prescribe weight-training. However, when this is not possible, it is essential to study a text-book on the particular event or sport. If it is one of the many athletic movements, then the Amateur Athletic Association's booklets are of great help as they usually contain film-strip action analysis of the event. It is better still to consult a good athletic coach or to have the athlete demonstrate the movement.

The action is then divided into three main sections:

(i) Arms and shoulder action.
(ii) Trunk action.
(iii) Leg action.

Do not be deceived by the preliminary movements: you must concentrate on the part of the movement where the greatest force is exerted. Pick out this movement, check up the direction in which the line of force is applied and the angle of the body in relation to the line of effort or the line of force.

As an example, let us look at the shot-putter in Plate 37. Here we see the shot-putter has just released the shot. Let us try to find the arm and shoulder action of this event. A line is drawn showing the direction in which the shot is travelling, that is, the line of effort.

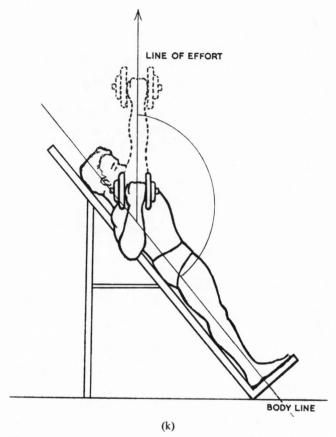

LINE OF EFFORT

BODY LINE

(k)

Another line is taken through the axis of the trunk and the angle between these two lines is noted.

Your next problem is to position the body so that the line of effort is now vertical without disturbing the angle between the line of effort and the body line. Diagram (k) shows the Alternate Dumb-bell Punching on an incline board, head high.

Here, we have positioned the athlete with two dumb-bells so that the line of action is similar to that part of the movement in the shot putt.

The trunk and leg action is then analysed and an exercise is chosen to supply a similar action over the same range of movement.

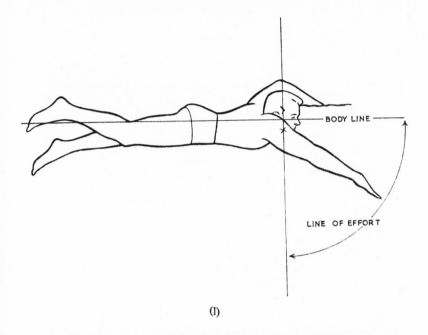

(l)

Actions which require a lot of effort in an upward direction are easy to analyse. For example, if one wished to develop the power of the leading leg in the high jump, fix an iron boot or leg-bell to the foot. Now assume a position similar to that when the leading leg begins the vigorous high kick upwards. Perform the same movement with a few sets of repetitions (say, 5 to 8) with suitable resistance.

This principle applies to all movements where the athlete applies force in the opposite direction to the downward pull of gravity.

Where the force is applied diagonally, horizontally or downwards then much more care must be exercised in the choice of starting position. Diagram (l) shows a swimmer in action. Here the resistance to be overcome is the water; the applied force by the muscles of the arms and shoulders is in a downward direction, so when applying dumb-bell or barbell exercises for assistance work in this instance, the body must be positioned as in the illustration. In this way, the arm and shoulder muscles are working in the same range of movement and at the same angle in relation to the body as when swimming. Diagram (m) shows the Declined Alternate Pull-overs with

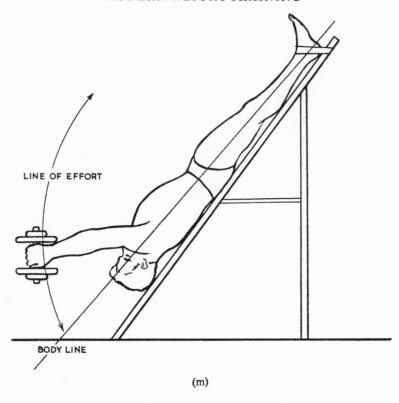

LINE OF EFFORT

BODY LINE

(m)

Dumb-bells exercise and it complies exactly with the principles we have discussed.

However, when springs or pulleys are used in the case of swimming, it is possible to position the body and the springs similar to that in the water. Bert Kinnear, national coach to the Amateur Swimming Association, is well aware of the values of these types of resistance and how the principles are applied, and his swimmers have derived great benefit from resistance training.

Massive Movements

After having spent weeks (or months) on the specific movements, excellent results can be obtained by concentrating on a crash pro-gramme to exercise the larger muscle groups involved in whatever event or sport is under discussion.

Massive movements are those exercises, such as the Olympic lifts, the Heave Press Overhead with Barbell or Dumb-bells, side flexion, trunk rotation, extension or flexion movements which incorporate the assistance of the arms, legs and back muscles.

High Pull-ups, Standing-Cleans with Barbells or Dumb-bells, Leaping Squats, Back Squats, Front Squats and Split Squats are all massive movement exercises which tie up and co-ordinate with the groups which have previously been exercised individually in the specific stage.

However, the athlete can return periodically to the specific or general stage of training from time to time depending on the position of his or her competitive season. The athlete must also vary from time to time the number of sets, repetitions and resistance used.

Basically, an athlete needing endurance, like a Marathon runner, can for example obtain excellent results from a short-period power schedule as used by the field-event man using the training principles involving heavy weights, fewer repetitions and several sets.

When the field-event man begins his weight-training after a hectic season, he can obtain worthwhile benefits by following a short fitness schedule (say, three to four weeks) on movements of light resistance which will permit more repetitions (in the 10 to 20 region) and two to three sets.

This will improve his cardio-vascular fitness prior to the heavy resistance schedules which are his normal training routine.

CHAPTER 9

WEIGHT-TRAINING AND ITS ADAPTATION TO ATHLETICS

A problem common to most athletes, even those who know and reap the benefits of weights, is how to fit in weight-training with their normal athletic season.

The quiet or closed season is the best time to introduce weight-training. In this way it will not interfere in any way with performance and it will also give the athlete time to study the subject and its particular problems.

Assuming the athlete has followed the advice in Chapter 8, he has spent several weeks on basic training and then passed on to specific weight-training for his event.

As the season approaches, he can cut down on his work output. This can be done by reducing:

(*a*) The number of exercises.

(*b*) The sets of repetition.

(*c*) The repetitions.

(*d*) The training periods.

Here is the breakdown of a specimen programme:

(i) *Start of closed or quiet season*
Normal basic schedule to last three to six weeks (three periods weekly).

(ii) *Specific schedule* of 3 to 6 exercises performing 3 to 5 sets on each exercise (three periods weekly).

(iii) *Four to eight weeks before season starts*
Select 3 to 5 power exercises, performing not more than 4 sets of 5 repetitions.

(iv) *Start of season*
Cut the number of exercises down to 4.

(v) *Season in full swing*
Divide your 4-exercise schedule by doing 2 exercises on a Tuesday and the others on a Thursday.

(vi) *Middle of season*
Select a good general power exercise, and on a Tuesday perform 4 or 5 sets of low repetitions. Select another power movement for Thursday and again carry out the 4 or 5 sets of low repetitions.

NOTE:

Some athletes, due to their fitness, recovery rate, or to some extent their event, can carry out a much heavier programme right through the season.

Several top athletes are satisfied to do 5 sets of 5 repetitions of High Pull-ups on a Monday and 5 sets of 5 repetitions of Upward Leaps with a barbell on a Wednesday. This is often enough to keep a fair degree of power building up to a more concentrated close-season programme.

CHAPTER 10

ISOMETRIC MUSCLE WORK

Although isometric contractions were briefly discussed in the chapter on kinetics, so much has been written recently on the subject I feel a chapter dealing exclusively with this would not be out of place.

Professor Mueller of Germany has probably done more research into the subject than anyone else. However, most of his research has been for the benefit of industry and the medical profession, and so far we have not witnessed any sensational results in the sports world. Nevertheless, I am convinced that there is a place in sport for such work provided it is applied correctly.

APPLICATION

Muscles can be exercised while holding a static position in which the position is held against varying degrees of resistance without joint movement, or:

(a) Where the muscles are applying force of varying degrees against an immovable object.

(b) Where full force is applied against an immovable object.

CONTRACTIONS AND TIME

The period of time these isometric contractions are held varies depending on the views of the experts. Most agree, however, that the period should range from four to eight seconds. They also agree that it is advisable to hold this contraction in a given position not more than once daily.

PRINCIPLES GOVERNING BODY POSITION

Having selected the action or part of the body to be strengthened, we revert once more to the use of full-range movement and its three sections—outer, inner and middle range. If time and energy are a problem, then select the mid-point of the middle range of each part to be exercised (the one-stage system). Plate 20 shows the exerciser applying full force at the mid-point of full-range elbow flexion. Should you be more ambitious, you can apply the Two-Stage System, whereby two positions are selected from the full range of

21.—The One-Stage System in isometric muscle work shows the exerciser selecting the mid-position of the middle range in elbow flexion.

22.—He applies force against the resistor during the Front Squat in the first position of the Two-Stage System.

23.—The second positon for the Front Squat.

24.—The Three-Stage System:
first position.

25.—The Three-Stage System:
second position.

26.—The Three-Stage System:
third position.

27.—A second example of the Three-Stage System showing the first position where force is applied against the resistor during the High Pull-up.

28.—The second position.

29.—The third position.

30.—Here is an exception to the general rule where the elbows are furthest from the shoulder fulcrum—in the One-Stage System.

31.—Al Murray adjusts the resistor which Mike Pearman is working on. This is done simply by altering the bar hook to a different link in the chain.

32.—Swimming is probably a sport where weight-training is introduced at an earlier age than in any other sport. Margaret Edwards is one of the many swimmers who have benefitted from Bert Kinnear's work with weight-training.

33.—A class of B.A.W.L.A. coaches is shown the technique of Olympic lifts by Al Murray in the grounds of the C.C.P.R.'s Bisham Abbey.

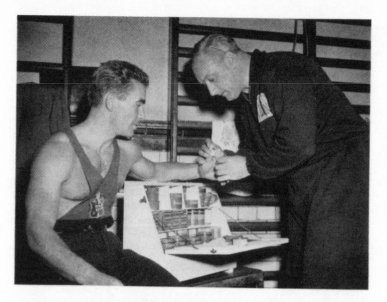

34.—Great care has to be taken of the hands when lifting. Here, Al Murray puts plaster on one of his pupils before a big lift is attempted.

35.—The road serves as the blackboard for Al Murray as he illustrates a point during one of his regular courses for B.A.W.L.A. coaches at Bisham Abbey, On the left of Wally Holland, secretary of the Coaching Scheme.

36.—Al Murray demonstrates the Two Hands Snatch to his class at the Gymnasium. Third on the left and the extreme right are former British Empire champions George Newton and Carl Goring.

37.—In 1949 Al Murray coached Mahmoud Namdjou of Iran for the world weightlifting championships. Here they talk tactics during a break in training. Namdjou went on to win the world bantam-weight title.

LINE OF EFFORT

ANGLE BETWEEN
LINE OF EFFORT
AND BODYLINE

U.L.A.C

BODY LINE

38.—This picture of Dr M. Lucking, past British Empire champion
shot-putter, illustrates the arm and shoulder action of this event
(see Chapter 8).

whatever action is selected for strength development. Here are the possible variations of isometric contractions:

(a) First position is at the junction of the outer and middle third of full range as in (21) Front Squat.

(b) The second position at the junction of the middle and inner range as in (22) Front Squat.

(c) Probably the most popular is the Three-Stage System. The first position is at the mid-point of the outer range, the second is at the mid-point of the middle range and the third position at the mid-point of the inner range.

The illustrations show how the positions can be changed.

THE ADVANTAGES OF ISOMETRIC WORK

(a) Muscles can be worked strongly with the minimum amount of time and effort.

(b) In the case of certain types of injury, the muscles can be worked without joint movement, which often reduces pain. Blood can be brought to the affected part with the minimum of discomfort which greatly assists the recovery rate.

(c) An athlete, consciously or subconsciously afraid of high poundages can exert full force without fear.

(d) For the non-athlete, isometric muscle work offers real advantages, especially when he must travel a great deal or where he has limited time or space for exercise. By selecting two positions for six major movements, holding each contraction for five seconds, his actual working time would not exceed *60 seconds daily.*

Imagine this for a moment. All the major muscles of the body can be strengthened with less than one minute's work a day. In fact, if you followed the routine only every other day, you would be more than pleased with the results.

SOME DISADVANTAGES OF ISOMETRIC WORK

With isometric work, one cannot see progress in the same way as with weights. This lack of motivation has been partly overcome in David Webster's 'Isodyne', a meter showing units indicating to the exerciser the force applied, also equipped with a light which goes on when the set poundage is reached during the contraction. All types of movement can be performed on this apparatus.

Many types of racks are made so that the exerciser can position the bar suitably to exercise any part of the body in almost any range. Some of these, however, are too expensive for the individual. The simplest type of isometric exerciser is a wooden base plate, barbell rod and chain connecting both, the chain allowing the height to be adjusted. As stated before, there is a lack of motivation here and secondly I believe that when *full force* is applied to an immovable object injury may occur, especially in the lower back.

Therefore, the addition of a powerful spring attached to the base and connected to the chain gives sufficiently to allow a small amount of movement at the start, and a certain resilience of movement during the isometric contraction. The fact that you can feel the springs slightly stretch on leg and back movements encourages the exerciser to greater efforts. Such a spring has been incorporated in my Isometric Resistors (see plates 20–30).

If you intend to combine this work with normal barbell training, introduce not more than 48 seconds of actual isometric work every second day.

If you do no other form of apparatus work, then 60 seconds of actual isometric work can be performed every day as I have said already. However, the addition of Upward Leaps, Sit-ups without resistance, and Press-ups on the floor or between two chairs can go a long way to providing you with strength and power, all with the minimum of time and effort.

The remaining photographs of the Isometric Resistor show some of the positions in which one can exercise by applying force at a given point of any movement by using one of the three systems described previously.

The One-Stage System. (20) shows the exerciser using the One-Stage System of selecting the mid-position of the middle range in elbow flexion.

The Two-Stage System. In (21) the exerciser applies force against the Resistor during the Front Squat in the first position of the Two-Stage System; in (22) he uses the second position for the Front Squat.

The Three-Stage System. By now, you should be able to recognize the first position in (23), the second in (24) and the third in (25). However, the first position can be set a little lower and the third a little higher to create wider gaps between the stages.

As a second example of the Three-Stage System, (26) shows the first position where force is applied against the resistor during the High Pull-up. The exerciser is at the second position in (27) and at the third in (28).

Reverting to the One-Stage System, I should add that in certain cases the best positions are at the final stage of movement rather than the mid-stage. Such an exception to the general rule is shown in (29) where the elbows are furthest from the shoulder fulcrum—the most difficult mechanically.

Finally in (30) I adjust the Resistor which Mike Pearman is working on. This is done simply by altering the bar hook to a different link in the chain.

Most suitable for club work is the larger model which employs a longer bar and baseboard, with chain and heavy spring attachment. With the latter model, practically every barbell exercise can be used.

The ultimate in isometric machines has been constructed by Dr A. Cameron and myself which enables the exerciser to perform isometric contractions in practically every position.

A meter shows the exact force exerted in pounds. This machine is also a first-class piece of apparatus for testing the individual's power in different positions at any point of full range.

Research on Isometric maximum effort has shown that this form of exercise is best avoided by those in the older age groups, who could possibly be hypertensive (suffering from high blood pressure), and by those greatly overweight and any suffering from any type of cardiovascular disease.

CHAPTER 11

TRAINING FOR STRENGTH, POWER AND SPEED

The lay public, and even to this day many coaches and athletes, talk of strength and power as if they were the same quality. Although closely related, it is better to have a clear picture of strength, power and speed as three separate qualities.

Strength is the ability to overcome resistance without the assistance of speed, momentum or technique.

Power is strength plus speed. It is the ability to move resistance at a relatively high speed.

Speed is the ability to move the body or part of the body or some outside resistance at a rate far greater than the normal speed of movement.

To illustrate the point, a dock worker might have the reputation of being very powerful. In fact, he may possess a far greater degree of strength than power. Now let's analyse these relative properties.

Strength

Examples of strength are the force exerted on such tests as a back or grip dynamometer, isometric contractions on an isometric rack or resistor as shown in Plates 20–30. In each case, force is applied against an almost immovable object or to hold a weight in a fixed position. Other examples are the lifting of extremely heavy weights through a very short range.

This might sound like a rather raw and uninteresting human quality, but I can assure you it is a very necessary one. However, the degree to which it should be developed depends on the requirements in your particular vocation, sport or hobby.

Power

Relies on two main factors:

(*a*) Strength.

(*b*) Speed—that is, the speed of muscular contractions naturally inherent or developed in the body to produce speed of movement against resistance.

The athlete who possesses real basic strength and has the natural gift of quick reactions and speed of muscular contraction will be able (even with heavy weights) to take full advantage of the favourable mechanical ranges present in most movements. Acceleration can be increased to assist in overcoming the resistance in the less favourable mechanical range. The slow-moving, slow-thinking person is at a distinct disadvantage when heavy resistance has to be overcome by power, that is, strength plus speed.

Examples of pure power should include as much speed as possible but a limited amount of technique. One would exclude such movements as the Two Hands Snatch despite the terrific amount of power required during the pull: too many other factors are involved, such as technique and balance, to make it a fair choice as an example of power.

Standing or Power Cleans, Pull-ups from the floor to arms' length (without leg dip), upwards leaping with heavy weights, heave presses with barbell or dumb-bells, cheating single-handed rowing, cheating curls and bench press, etc., give a clearer picture of power movements.[1]

Speed

So closely allied to power. When one thinks of speed, one visualizes a fast-moving athlete, usually one who overcomes light resistance at great speed. Even with light resistance, speed is dependent on strength to a certain degree. Geoff Dyson, one of the greatest athletic coaches of our time, continually stresses the fact that no matter how light the resistance to be overcome on a speed event, the athlete should become much stronger than the event would indicate.

Food for thought comes in the shot or hammer events, performed by top field men. When using the junior shot or hammer he can throw it further, simply because the lighter resistance permits greater speed of movement supplied by the power available.

Should it be possible for the same athlete to maintain the same degree of technique, speed and fitness, etc., yet greatly increase his basic strength and power, it is therefore reasonable to assume that on his return to the normal weight of shot or hammer, the greater resistance to be overcome will now feel proportionately lighter than it did before the experiment.

The increase in strength and power should enable him to produce greater speed and movement and hence increase his throwing distance. This may sound over-simplified but is basically true.

[1] The upward part of all power movements should be performed as fast and fiercely as possible. Such movements as straight-arm pull-overs and straight-legged dead lifts are excepted; in these cases, the leverage is difficult and it calls for a more controlled movement.

CHAPTER 12

WEIGHT-TRAINING EQUIPMENT

The International Olympic Barbell

This is the official regulation equipment used in all weightlifting competitions including Olympic Games and World Championships.

To stand up to the tremendous strain, the bar should be in the region of 85-ton tensile steel. To each end of the bar, round discs (machined to fine limits to ensure exact weight) are added. In English-speaking countries, the discs are usually marked in pounds, but for international competitions, kilos are used.

These discs revolve on a special end sleeve which permits smooth and accurate movement. The discs are held in place by the special collar shown in the centre of Plate (4).

Exercise Barbells

Exercise barbells are simplified versions of the International Olympic set. They consist of a 1-in. diameter steel rod varying in length from 4 to 6 ft. A chromium-plated revolving centre sleeve prevents the discs from coming inwards and permits smooth execution. Fixing collars are attached to each outside end to prevent the discs from sliding off. This type of apparatus is used for most types of two-handed exercise.

Dumb-bells

Dumb-bells are a smaller version of the barbell and are used for single-handed exercises. The bar varies in length from 12 to 18 in. A short revolving centre grip prevents the discs from coming inwards. Small fixing collars are attached to the ends of the bar to prevent the disc from falling off.

Squat Stands

Squatting is an essential part of an athlete's training. The tremendous power that can be developed in the legs and back permits the athlete to use weights much heavier than he can place behind the neck by his own efforts. Therefore the bar, before loading, is placed on the stands just in front of the exerciser. The barbell is then loaded to the required poundage. The exerciser then ducks under the bar, by bending the knees and then straightens his legs, raising the barbell clear off the stands, steps back one pace and performs his knee bending as in Plate (5). The reverse procedure is adopted when the exercise is finished.

Leg Pressing Machine

Although the exercise known as the Leg Press appears similar to that of squatting, the resistance is thrown on different parts of the leg and hips. This piece of apparatus has a base on which the exerciser lays, placing his feet under the cross bar which slides up and down on two vertical tubes. Weights up to 700 lb. or more can be loaded on to this simple type of apparatus. As knee and lower back injuries can occur, the Leg Pressing Machine is invaluable in aiding their recovery. This is due to the fact that it does not throw the resistance on to the same muscles as used in heavy squatting, Plates (6 and 7).

Calf Machine

To the layman, this might look a complicated piece of apparatus merely to develop the efficiency and size of the calfs. However, when the exerciser merely performs Heel Raising with the barbell resting across the shoulders, a great deal of cheating (see Chapter 5) can occur. The exerciser, when he is about to raise the heels, leans slightly forward and this alone assists the muscles at the back of the lower leg to raise the heels.

However, when this machine is used the block for the toes can be moved forwards so that the shoulders are horizontally behind the toes. When the exerciser raises the heels, there is no forward or backward movement of the body to assist the calf muscles. The weight is attached to a lever which rotates at a fulcrum near the vertical upright. Therefore, tremendous resistance can be produced with a comparatively light weight, Plates (8 and 9).

Adjustable Long Inclined Bench

This is a specially designed piece of apparatus which can change the angle of many exercises, for it is as well to remember that, 'to alter the starting position of an exercise is to alter the effects'. The exerciser can exercise with his feet at the top, fixed by straps, or he can lie on the board with his feet on the base support performing all types of barbell and dumb-bell exercises, Plates (10 and 11).

CHAPTER 13

MAJOR WEIGHT-TRAINING EXERCISES

In this chapter I have explained a large number of basic and specific exercises with full illustrations.

Two types of athletes have been used to demonstrate the exercises. The athlete in the first section is Danny Donovan, an all-round lifter, weight-trainer, rugby player and staff instructor to the B.A.W.L.A. He represents the sportsman who lifts not only to improve his particular sport but also for the general fitness which results from it.

In the second section I have used Mike Pearman—English Native Middleweight Champion of 1962—to illustrate my points that great weights can be handled using maximum power *without* being heavily muscled. Mike is a young International Olympic lifter of whom I expect great things in the years to come.

However, for the reader who just wants massive development, the earlier chapter on Schedule Construction will be the answer.

NOTE. After the early exercises in which simple terms are used, correct anatomical names are introduced to accustom the reader to these.

GET SET

Starting Position (38). Grip the bar, knuckles to the front, shoulders slightly forward, head up and eyes looking to the front. Arms are straight, the back is flat but not vertical. Insteps under the bar.

This is the correct starting position you should assume when lifting a weight from the floor. It is also important that you should finish in this position when returning the bar to the floor.

39

THE HIGH PULL-UP

Starting Position. Assume starting position. Get Set.

Movement. Pull the bar high as in (40). Note the position of the wrists and elbow, also the position of the chest—it is high and the hips are slightly forward as the body comes up high on the toes. Repeat in a brisk, non-stop rhythm. (41) shows the mid-way position. Note: the elbows are directed sideways.

Breathing. Breathe in as you raise the bar, and out as you lower to the starting position.

Purpose. With light weights this movement is useful as a warming-up exercise.

However, with heavier weights it is a real all-round power builder.

40

41

Starting Position (42). Chin held in, chest high, the bar is held on the chest and the heel of the hand, forearms a little in advance of the bar, hips slightly forward. The bar, hip joints and insteps are in one vertical line.

Movement. Press the bar straight to arms' length with the body kept quite still. Make a special effort to hold the chest high (43).

Breathing. Breathe in as you drive the bar overhead , and out as you return the bar to the chest.

Purpose. To develop the shoulders, upper back and muscles at the rear of the upper arm.

Note: this exercise must not be confused with the more complicated technique of the Olympic Press.

TWO HANDS CURL

Starting Position (44). Note the body is vertical, arms straight and palms to the front.

Movement. Bend the arms strongly at the elbows until the bar rests on the chest as in (45). Make sure that the bar is kept close to the body.

Finishing Position (45). Note that the elbows are fully flexed, yet still behind the bar, thus keeping the resistance on the muscles concerned. Should you bring the elbows forward and upwards, you will take all the resistance away and defeat the object of the exercise.

By varying the grip on the bar from a wide grip to a very close one, or by changing the position of the trunk, the effect of the exercise can be altered.

Breathing. Breathe in as you raise the bar and out as you lower it.

Purpose. To develop the muscle on the front of the upper arm.

TWO HANDS PRESS

42

43

TWO HANDS CURL

44

45

Starting Position (46). Feet are comfortably apart, normally hip width, with the bar resting across the upper back. (The heels may be raised on blocks of wood, $1\frac{1}{2}$ in. high).

Movement. Bend the knees and squat down as low as in (47), gently rebound out of the low position and rise strongly by lifting the head; at the same time strongly straightening the legs.

Low Position. The back is flat, but not vertical. This position elevates the ribs and has a stretching effect on the thorax, which encourages chest growth. The Squat can be used with many variations for the legs, or as a general power builder. Due to the larger groups of muscles being used, a great demand is made on the circulatory and respiratory systems, which greatly encourages increasing body weight. The Squat is the keystone of many body-building schedules. Should you find difficulty in keeping the back flat as you approach the low position, it is advisable either to avoid going all the way down or to put a block of wood under the heels about $1\frac{1}{2}$ in. high. This throws most of the resistance on the front of the thighs.

The effects of this exercise can be greatly altered by the extent to which the exerciser bends his legs. Several hundred pounds can be used in shallow or half squats.

Breathing. Fill the lungs, bend the knees, breathe out just as you rebound in the low position and you will find the air is driven out of the lungs, Breathe in as you rise.

Purpose. To develop the legs, back and chest, and to improve the condition of the heart and lungs. Note: in most cases it is neither necessary nor advisable to go lower than in (47).

PRESS ON BENCH

Starting Position ((48). Back-lying, on bench. Bar resting on the chest, forearms vertical below the bar, hands wide apart.

Movement. Press the barbell vigorously to arms' length, until you reach the position in (49).

Breathing. Breathe in as you press the bar upwards and out as you return it to the chest.

Purpose. To develop the chest muscles, front shoulder muscles and muscles on the back of the upper arm.

Variation of this exercise can be performed by supporting the bar across the lower chest, hands shoulder-width apart, arms close to the side of the chest. This variation throws a greater resistance on the arms and shoulders.

THE SQUAT
(OR FULL KNEE BEND)

46

47

PRESS ON
BENCH

48

49

Starting Position. Assume position in (50). Note the arms are straight and the chest is held high.

Movement. Round the spine and bend forward from the hips until your barbell touches the ground. In the early stages, the knees can be very slightly bent.

Low Position (51). When this exercise is performed correctly with a light weight it adds greatly to the mobility of the spine. When lowering from the starting position, begin by lowering the head first, followed by rounding the shoulders and upper back. In other words, make sure you round the spine as a whole. When recovering, attempt to straighten up the lower spine first: the head should be the last part to be raised to the erect position. It is advisable to progress slowly with this particular exercise.

Breathing. Breathe out as you lower the bar, and in as you return the bar to the starting position.

Purpose. To develop the muscles which extend the spine and hip joints, the hip muscles and the hamstring group at the back of the upper leg.

Variation. The above exercise can be performed with a flat back and feet astride. This throws all the resistance on to the lower back, hip and hamstrings (muscles behind the thigh).

BENT-FORWARD ROWING

Starting Position. Assume position in (52). Note that the back is flat, head up, arms straight, knuckles to the front, hands fairly wide apart, feet wide astride, knees slightly bent.

Movement. Pull the bar strongly to the chest, by bending the arms and raising the elbows sideways (53).

Raised Position (53). This shows the position as the bar touches the top of the chest. It is an excellent exercise for improving shoulder posture. Note that the body has not moved during the movement.

Breathing. Breathe in as the bar is pulled to the chest, and out as the weight is returned to the starting position.

Purpose. Principally to develop the upper back muscles. The effects of this exercise can be altered by bringing the bar up and back to touch the lower abdomen, this affects the lower back muscles.

STRAIGHT-LEGGED DEAD LIFT

50

51

BENT-FORWARD ROWING

52

53

Starting Position. Assume the position in (54), keeping the hands 6 to 8 in. apart.

Movement. Pull the bar strongly upwards, by bending the elbows and raising them sideways. Keep the body still throughout. (55) shows the bar near completion of the movement.

Breathing. Breathe in on the upward movement and out as you return the bar to the starting position.

Purpose. To develop the upper back muscles, and the muscles on the front of the upper arms.

Variation. Pull the barbell towards the lower abdomen.

HEELS RAISING

Starting Position. Bar resting on the shoulders behind as in (56). Toes, and the ball of the foot each resting on a raised base. This can be a piece of wood about 12 in. long and 4 in. × 2 in. thick. This will allow a full range of movement at the ankle.

Movement. Lower the heels until they rest on the floor, reach high on your toes. Later, you can make this exercise more effective by dropping the heels to touch the floor and rebounding straight back into the position shown in (56).

Breathing. Breathe in as you raise the body upwards, and out on the downward movement.

Purpose. To develop the calf muscles.

CLOSE-GRIP BENT-FORWARD ROWING

54

55

**HEELS
RAISING**

56

Starting Position. Back-lying on a narrow bench. The barbell is held at arms' length as in (57).

Movement. Keep the arms straight and lower the bar in a quarter circle backwards until you reach the position shown in (58), or even lower down.

Stretch Position (58). In the early stages, it is advisable to keep the lower back flat on the bench, and the wieght light. A good point to remember in all straight-arm movements is the advisibility of performing the first two repetitions in slow, steady time to make sure the muscles are stretched over the full range, before you attempt the exercise at full tempo.

Breathing. Breathe in as you lower the bar, and out as you return to the starting position.

Purpose. To enlarge the thorax and develop muscles surrounding the shoulder girdle, also the muscles on the front of the chest and the large muscles of the lower back.

Variation. The bar may be started from a resting place across the thighs.

BENT-ARM PULL-OVER

Starting Position. Back-lying on a bench or form, bar resting on the lower chest as in (59), but with narrow grip and elbows at the sides.

Movement. Raise the bar off the chest and directly backwards over the head until it reaches the position shown in (60). Try to keep the elbow joints at right angles throughout the movement.

Breathing. Breathe in as the bar goes backwards, and out as you return the bar to the chest.

Purpose. To stretch and mobilize the thorax, and to develop the chest muscles and the large muscles of the lower back.

Variation. A centrally loaded dumb-bell may be used.

57 STRAIGHT-ARM PULL-OVER

58

59

BENT-ARM PULL-OVER

60

Starting Position. Bend down, grip the bar knuckles to the front, hands approximately 8 in. apart and stand up. The bar should now be hanging at arms' length against the top of the thighs. This is the starting position (61).

Movement. Pull the bar up the front of the body until it reaches the height of the chin (62).

Breathing. Breathe in as the bar is raised and out as you return it to the starting position.

Purpose. To develop the muscles surrounding the shoulders and upper back, also the muscle which flexes the elbow.

Variation. Cheating version, the legs may be used slightly to assist the exerciser to handle heavier weights.

DUMB-BELL PRESS

Starting Position. Grip two dumb-bells, one in each hand, bring the bells to the shoulders as in (63).

Movement. Press the dumb-bells evenly to arms' length overhead, keeping the body in the starting position throughout. As you drive the bells from the shoulder, lift the chest high (64).

Finishing Position. The chest is held high and the body is in a strong upright position with the elbows straight and the arms vertical. Dumb-bell work has a very strengthening effect on the muscles, especially on the overhead exercises as they are much more difficult to control than the barbell.

Breathing. Breathe in as the bells are pressed overhead and out as the bells are returned to the starting position.

Purpose. To develop the shoulder muscles, upper back muscles and the muscle at the back of the upper arm.

UPRIGHT ROWING

61

62

DUMB-BELL PRESS

63

64

Starting Position. Back-lying on a narrow bench or form. Dumb-bells are held at arms' length vertically over the shoulders (65).

Movement. Keep the arms straight, lower the bells sideways until they are approximately below the level of the shoulders, this is the straight-arm version of the lateral raise lying. Comparatively light weights must be used for this exercise (66).

Breathing. Breathe in as the bells are lowered and out as the bells are returned to the starting position (65).

Purpose. To develop the chest muscles and muscles on the front of the shoulder.

BENT-ARM LATERAL RAISE LYING

Starting Position. Assume position in (66).

Movement. Lower the bells sideways, keeping the arms straight. During the first part of this movement allow the elbows to bend when the resistance becomes too great until you reach the position in (67) or lower still. Note the bells are well outside the elbows in the low position (in the bent-arm version of the lateral raise lying). Much more weight can be handled this way; of course this is for advanced weight trainers only.

Breathing. Breathe in as the bells are lowered and out as you return to the starting position illustrated in (66).

Purpose. To develop the chest muscles, and the muscles on the front of the shoulders.

65

**STRAIGHT-ARM
LATERAL RAISE
LYING**

66

67

**BENT-ARM
LATERAL
RAISE
LYING**

Starting Position. Standing erect, feet a few inches apart. Dumb-bells hanging at arms' length as in (68) with rear end of the disc resting against the front of the thighs. Note the grip with knuckles facing outwards. This starting position prevents the exerciser from swinging the bells at the start of the movement.

Movement. Bend the arms strongly at the elbows, as the bells reach the midway position, turn the rear ends in towards each other. Keep the elbows from coming too far forwards at the completion of the curl (69).

Finishing Position (69). The body is erect and the elbows are still behind the bell; this is important to keep the resistance on the muscles being used.

Breathing. Breathe in as the weights are raised and out as you return to the starting position.

Purpose. To develop the muscles of the front of the upper arm.

SIDE TO SIDE BEND

Starting Position. Stand astride a dumb-bell, bend down and pick it up with the right hand, and assume the position in (70). Keep the body square to the front.

Movement. Bend the body strongly to the left and endeavour to reach even further to the left than illustrated in (71).

Finishing Position (71). Note how the body has kept to the lateral plane. The exerciser should again attempt to reach further than shown here. This is an excellent exercise for reducing the waist-line.

Breathing. Breathe in as you raise the weight and out as you return to the starting position.

Purpose. To develop the muscles on the sides of the trunk and numerous other muscles surrounding the mid-section.

DUMB-BELL SCREW CURL

68

69

SIDE TO SIDE BEND

70

71

Starting Position. Back-lying, dumb-bells held as in (72). Note the backward angle of the arms and the tilt back of the bells. The bells are supported by the little finger side of the hand resting against the inside of the front disc.

Movement. Keep the upper arm still as you lower the bells into the position as in (73). Drive the bells straight back to the starting position, making sure the bells never come vertically over the shoulders. This keeps the resistance on the triceps muscles.

Lower Position. Care should be taken in lowering the bells from the positions in (72) and (73). Note the elbows are well bent and pointed high. The hands are close to the inside of the front discs.

Breathing. Breathe in as the bells are raised and out as they are lowered.

Purpose. To develop the muscles at the back of the upper arm.

Variation. Cheating version, the dumb-bells may be lowered further than illustrated in (73) and the upper arm can assist the start of the movement.

SEATED DUMB-BELL CURL

Starting Position. Take one dumb-bell, sit down and place the dumb-bell as in (74). Note the angle of the arm, also the position of the right knee. This prevents any backward movement of the upper arm and isolates the movement to the flexors of the elbow.

Movement. Strongly bend the arm until the elbow is fully flexed. The rest of the body is kept still as in (75).

Finishing Position. Once you take up position as in (75) make sure that the movement is confined to the elbow only. Pull the head back and turn the chin slightly away from the bell to allow full flexion of the elbow. Owing to the static position of the rest of the body, the flexors of the elbow are forced to work hard throughout the movement, and especially when the flexors are working in the inner range.

Breathing. Breathe is as the bell is raised and out as it is lowered to the starting position.

Purpose. To develop the muscles on the front of the upper arm.

TRICEP BENCH PRESS WITH DUMB-BELLS

72

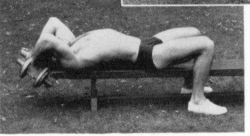

73

SEATED DUMB-BELL CURL

74

75

Starting Position. Feet astride with the bar resting comfortably behind the neck as in (76).

Movement. Press the barbell straight to arms' length overhead as in the finishing position shown in (77).

Breathing. Breathe in on the upward movement and out as you return to the starting position.

Purpose. To develop the upper back muscles, muscles of the shoulder and those at the rear of the upper arm.

STANDING TRICEP PRESS WITH DUMB-BELL

Starting Position. Feet astride with the dumb-bell lowered behind the neck as in the position (78).

Movement. Vigorously straighten the elbow until you finish as in (79).

Breathing. Breathe in as the dumb-bell is raised and out as it is lowered.

Purpose. To develop the muscles at the rear of the upper arm.

WALK STANDING, HEEL RAISING

Starting Position. Assume the position in (80). Note that one foot is a short step in advance of the other as in walking. The ball of the foot is on a raised base (either in the form of a disc or piece of wood) and $1\frac{1}{2}$ in. high. This provides a greater range of movement.

Movement. Lower the heels to touch the ground and immediately return to the starting position (80).

Breathing. Breathe freely throughout the exercise.

Purpose. Develop the calf muscles.

PRESS BEHIND NECK

77

76

STANDING TRICEP PRESS WITH DUMB-BELL

78

79

80

WALK STANDING, HEEL RAISING

Starting Position. Stand with the feet a little apart with the heels on two discs, each about $1\frac{1}{2}$ in. high, with the bar grasped behind the thighs as in (81).

Movement. Lower the bar to the ground behind the legs as in (82), making sure you lean slightly forwards from the hips to counterbalance the weight as you bend the knees.

Breathing. Breathe out as you lower the weight and in as you assume the starting position.

Purpose. To develop the leg and hip muscles.

SINGLE-ARM ROWING

Starting Position. Feet astride, legs bent, one hand supported on a low bench. The dumb-bell hangs vertically beneath the shoulder as in (83).

Movement. Pull the dumb-bell strongly from the position in (83) to that in (84).

Breathing. Breathe in as the bell is raised and out as you return to the starting position.

Purpose. To develop the upper back muscles, the trunk and muscles on the front of the upper arm.

HACK LIFT

81

82

SINGLE-ARM ROWING

83

84

Starting Position. Assume feet stride position with the bar resting comfortably behind the neck as in (85).

Movement. Bend forwards from the hips, keeping the back flat, but allow the knees to bend slightly as the trunk comes horizontal to the ground as in (86).

Breathing. Breathe out as you bend forwards and in as you return to the starting position.

Purpose. To develop the muscles at the rear of thigh, hips and lower back muscles.

BENT-ARM LATERAL RAISE STANDING WITH DUMB-BELLS

Starting Position. Assume the feet astride position in (87) with the dumb-bells pointing forwards and upwards. The rear disc should rest on the thigh with the arms slightly bent.

Movement. Raise the dumb-bells forward and sideways as in (88). Raise the chest high at the same time. Lower and repeat the movement.

Breathing. Breathe in as you raise the bells and out as they return to the starting position.

Purpose. To develop the shoulder and upper back muscles.

TRUNK FORWARD BEND

85

86

BENT-ARM LATERAL RAISE STANDING
WITH DUMB-BELLS

87

88

BENT FORWARD TRICEP PRESS
WITH DUMB-BELLS

Starting Position. Feet astride, knees bent. Lower the chest to rest on the upper thighs, elbows pointing upwards as in (89)

Movement. Hold position (89) and extend both elbows as in (90). The body, and shoulders are to be kept still during the movement.

Breathing. Breathe freely throughout the movement.

Purpose. To develop the muscles at the rear of the upper arm.

SEE-SAW PRESS WITH DUMB-BELLS
(Also known as the Side to Side Press with Dumb-bells)

Starting Position. Feet astride with the dumb-bells held at the shoulders, as in (91).

Movement. Begin the movement with a press upwards with the weaker arm first. Strict attention must be paid to the trunk action, the exercise finishing in the position (92).

Breathing. Breathe as freely as possible during the movement.

Purpose. To develop the shoulder, upper back, waist and muscles at the rear of the upper arm.

BENT FORWARD TRICEP PRESS
WITH DUMB-BELLS

89

90

SEE-SAW PRESS WITH DUMB-BELLS

91

92

Starting Position. Assume position in (93).

Movement. Kick with the outside leg upwards, vigorously, to reach position (94). As you kick, allow the inner, supporting leg to bend a little. Turn round and repeat the exercise with the other foot.

Breathing. Breathe out as you kick and in as you lower the leg.

Purpose. To develop the abdominal muscles and those that cross the front of the hip joint—also the front of thigh muscles.

CHEATING SINGLE-ARM ROWING

Starting Position. Take up position in (95), keeping the back as flat as possible.

Movement. Pull the dumb-bell vigorously up into position (96). Rotate the trunk so that the chest is facing sideways and upwards. Keep the free hand on a low chair or stool. This should not be higher than 1 ft above the floor.

Breathing. In as you raise the dumb-bell and out as you return to the starting position.

Purpose. To develop the muscles which rotate the trunk, also those of the shoulder and upper back.

HIGH KICK WITH LEGBELL

93

94

CHEATING SINGLE-ARM ROWING

95

96

Starting Position. Assume the position as in (97).

Movement. Pull upwards and sideways with the trunk, passing through position (98) until you come to finish in (99), simulating the basic movement of the shot-putter.

Breathing. Breathe in as you lift the weight from the ground and out as you return to the starting position.

Purpose. To develop the muscles responsible for sideways movements of the trunk, and to a lesser degree those muscles which rotate the spine.

LEVERAGE SIDE BEND

Starting Position. Having loaded a barbell with weights at one end, take up the position in (100).

Movement. Bend the trunk strongly away from the weight, attempt to touch the outside of the thigh with the elbow furthest from the weight (101).

Breathing. Breathe as freely as the movement permits.

Purpose. To develop the lateral flexors of the spine.
Note. This leverage bell principle can be applied to many exercises.

SHOT SIDE BEND

97   98   99

LEVERAGE SIDE BEND

100   101

INCLINED BENCH LEG-RAISING WITH TRUNK TWISTING

Starting Position. Assume the position in (102).

Movement. Raise both legs from position (102) until the feet are vertically over the face, now lower the legs as far sideways as possible, shown in (103). Return by the same route to position (102).

Breathing. It is advisable to breathe as freely as possible during the twist but breathe out as the legs are raised. This is one of the exceptions to the general rule.

Purpose. To develop the abdominal muscles, spinal flexors and rotators.

INCLINED LEG-RAISING

Starting Position. Assume the position shown in (102).

Movement. Raise both legs together until you reach a position somewhere near to that in (104). The knees can be slightly unlocked. The bench can be lowered nearly to the horizontal position if the above exercise proves too tough initially.

Breathing. Breathe out as you raise the legs and in as you return to the starting position.

Purpose. To develop the abdominal muscles, hip and spinal flexors.

INCLINED BENCH
LEG-RAISING WITH
TRUNK TWISTING

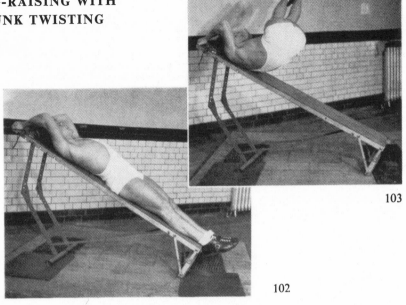

103

102

INCLINED
LEG-RAISING

104

Starting Position. Assume position (105), leaving the knees slightly bent.

Movement. Sit up, reaching forwards with the head in an attempt to touch the knees with the forehead. Allow the knees to bend a little more as you reach forwards, finishing in the position in (106).

Breathing. Breathe out as you sit up and reach forward, also breathe out as you return to the starting position.

Purpose. To develop the abdominal muscles (hip and spinal flexors).

ALTERNATIVE PRESSING ON INCLINED BENCH

Starting Position. Assume position in (107).

Movement. Start by punching the bell that is in the left hand upwards (108). As you bring it down, punch up the bar in the right hand, keeping up a rhythmic see-saw action.

Breathing. Breathe as freely as the action permits.

Purpose. To develop upward and forward punching (those muscles situated at the front of the shoulder and back of the upper arm).

INCLINED
SIT-UPS

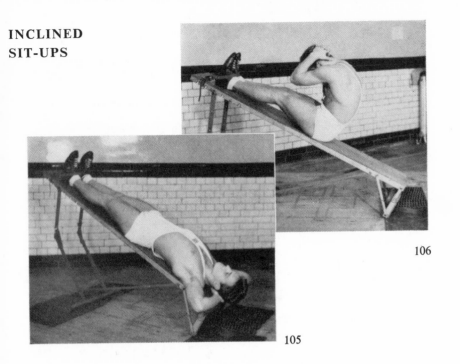

106

105

ALTERNATIVE PRESSING ON INCLINED BENCH

107

108

Starting Position. Assume (109) making sure the arms are in a position so that you can control the upward thrust.

Movement. Drive the dumb-bells vertically upwards into position (110).

Breathing. Breathe in on the way up and and out as you return to the starting position.

Purpose. To develop the extensors of the elbow, flexors of the shoulders and the abductors of the scapulae, muscles on the upper back, front of shoulder and rear of upper arm.

Variation. The dumb-bells in line instead of for and aft.

DECLINED BARBELL PRESS

Starting Position. Assume the position in (111). Ensure that the feet are securely fixed at the top of the bench. Note the position of the elbows in relation to the bar.

Movement. Press the barbell vertically upwards until the arms are straight as in (112).

Breathing. Breathe in on the way up and out as you return to the starting position.

Purpose. To develop the protractors (and to a lesser degree the depressors) of the shoulders, and the extensors of the elbows; also muscles situated at the front of shoulder and chest rear of upper arm.

Variation. A narrower or wider grip may be used.

DUMB-BELL INCLINED PRESS

109

110

DECLINED BARBELL PRESS

112

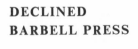

111

Starting Position. Clean the two dumb-bells from the floor to the shoulders, dip the body by bending both legs and assume the position in (113).

Movement. Drive the dumb-bells straight to arms' length, finishing in position (114). The last half of the movement should be carried out in good pressing form. Dumb-bells are more difficult to control and therefore build a certain ruggedness in the exerciser.

Breathing. Breathe in on the way up and out as you return to the starting position.

Purpose. To develop the same group of muscles as the Barbell Heave Press, i.e. to develop collectively power in the extensors of the arms and legs, also the shoulder flexors and the elevators of the shoulder girdle.

HEAVE PRESS WITH BARBELL

Starting Position. Pull the barbell from the floor to the chest, dip the body by bending the Press to assume the position in (115).

Movement. Extend the legs and arms vigorously, finish the last half of the movement in the correct pressing style, finishing as in (116).

Breathing. Breathe in as you extend the arms and legs and as you lower the bar to the starting position. As this is a power movement, it is often necessary to breathe in and out a few times between repetitions at the shoulder.

Purpose. To develop collectively power and development in the arms, shoulders and legs. Muscles: The extensors of the arms and legs; the shoulder flexors and elevators of the shoulder girdle.

HEAVE PRESS WITH TWO DUMB-BELLS

113

114

HEAVE PRESS WITH BARBELL

115

116

Starting Position. Assume position (117). Make sure that the legs are apart to ensure better balance and control. See that the bar rests solely on the chest with the arms positioned so that they can exert the greatest force.

Movement. Drive the bar verically upwards with the arms and shoulders until it reaches the position in (118).

Breathing. Breathe in forcibly as the bar leaves the chest and out as you return to the starting position.

Purpose. To develop the arm, shoulder and chest muscles.

Variation. A narrower or wider grip may be used.

INCLINED DUMB-BELL PRESS

Starting Position. Assume the position in (119). The effect of the exercise can be changed by turning the rear ends of the dumb-bells inwards so that they are in line.

Movement. Drive the dumb-bells upwards with the arms and shoulders until you reach the position in (120). Lower the bells and repeat the procedure.

Breathing. Breathe in on the upward movement and out as you return the dumb-bells to the starting position.

Purpose. To develop the elevators and abductors of the shoulder, and the extensors of the elbow.

Variation. The dumb-bells may be held in line instead of fore and aft.

INCLINED
BARBELL PRESS

117

118

INCLINED DUMB-BELL PRESS

119

120

Starting Position. Assume the position in (121).
Make sure balance is correct before making any attempt to lift the weight.

Movement. Drive the bar vertically upwards, keeping it close to the face and taking great care that the bar does not go backwards as it passes the top of the head. Finish in a good, strong, well-balanced position as in (122).

Breathing. Breathe in as the bar goes up and as you return to the position (121).

Purpose. The seated position of this exercise isolates the work, mainly to the arms and shoulders. It is therefore a good exercise to create power and development of the arm extensors and elevators of the shoulder girdle.

BENT-ARM PULL-OVER WITH SWINGBELL*

Starting Position. Assume position (123).

Movement. Lower the bell backwards and downwards, keeping it close to the head and bench. Reach backwards until the upper arms are nearly parallel with the bench as in (124).

Breathing. Breathe in as the bell goes backwards and out as you return to the starting position.

Purpose. To mobilize the thorax, and to develop the muscles surrounding the thorax.

* Centrally loaded dumb-bell.

SEATED PRESS WITH BARBELL

121

122

BENT-ARM PULL-OVER WITH SWINGBELL*

* Centrally loaded dumb-bell.

123

124

**CHEATING BENT-FORWARD
LATERAL RAISE STANDING**

Starting Position. Assume the position in (125), knees slightly bent and the back flat.

Movement. Use the legs to assist in starting the dumb-bells sideways, finishing in the position (126). This movement can also be performed in strict technique, without the assistance of the legs.

Breathing. Breathe in as you raise the bells and out as you return to the starting position.

Purpose. To develop the abductors of the scapulae and muscles which cap the shoulder joint.

BENT-FORWARD SWINGBELL CURL

Starting Position. Assume position as (127): try to maintain legs and back in the starting position throughout.

Movement. Bend the arms strongly, paying attention to keep the trunk and upper arm still throughout the movement. Make sure the elbows are fully flexed and behind the bell as in (128).

Breathing. Breathe in as the weight comes up and out as you lower to the starting position.

Purpose. To develop the flexors of the arm.

CHEATING BENT-FORWARD LATERAL RAISE STANDING

125

126

BENT-FORWARD SWINGBELL CURL

127

128

**BENT-ARM DECLINED LATERAL RAISE
WITH DUMB-BELLS**

Starting Position. Assume the position in (129).

Movement. Lower the arms sideways, keeping them straight until the midway position. They are then bent for the final half of the exercise, finishing in (130).

Breathing. Breathe in as you lower the dumb-bells and out as you return to the starting position.

Purpose. To develop the muscles on the front of the chest and shoulder joints.

**BENT-ARM INCLINED LATERAL RAISE
WITH DUMB-BELLS**

Starting Position. Assume position in (131).

Movement. Lower the dumb-bells sideways. Start with the arms straight, allowing them to bend midway through the movement, finishing in position (132).

Breathing. Breathe in as you lower and out as you return the dumb-bells to the starting position.

Purpose. To develop powerful abductors of the scapulae, and muscles on the front of the chest and shoulder joints.

BENT-ARM DECLINED LATERAL RAISE
WITH DUMB-BELLS

129

130

BENT-ARM INCLINED LATERAL RAISE
WITH DUMB-BELLS

131

132

Starting Position. Take up the position in (133) making sure that you are in a well-balanced position.

Movement. Leap upwards, putting as much effort as possible into the drive from the legs. Be sure to land on the toes. Bend the knees to take the shock out of landing (134).

Breathing. Breathe in as you leap and out as you land.

Purpose. This develops an explosive leg action, and also develops the muscles of the hips, front of thighs and calf muscles.

SPLIT SQUATS

Starting Position. Take up the position shown in (135). Make sure that your balance is perfect before attempting the movement.

Movement. Lower the body and the weight from position (135) to that in (136) by bending both legs. Note how the forward knee is in advance of the forward foot.

Breathing. Breathe as freely as possible during the exercise.

Purpose. To build power and mobility in the legs. The position of the forward thigh in this exercise is inwards and has a completely different effect from Front and Back Squats. This exercise activates most of the major leg muscles.

VERTICAL JUMPS

133

134

SPLIT SQUATS

135

136

Starting Position. Load the barbell on the squat stands. Grip the bar, bend the knees and raise the barbell clear of the stands.

Movement. Lower the body into position (137). Vigorously extend the legs and return to the upright standing position.

Breathing. Breathe out as you bend the knees and in as you rise to the standing position.

Purpose. To develop mainly the muscles on the front of the thigh and the hip muscles.

HALTING HIGH DEAD LIFT

Starting Position. Assume a good 'Get Set' position, standing right up with the weight. Now lower the weight into the starting position shown in (138). Remain in this position for 4 to 6 seconds. Keeping the head and shoulders in advance of the bar.

Movement. Swing the hips forward and upward as you extend the legs and flex the arms until you reach the position in (139). As the bar comes down, bend the legs; check the bar at the thighs and lower again into the position in (138). Repeat this whole movement, then lower the weight to the ground.

Breathing. Breathe as freely as possible throughout.

Purpose. To build real power, not only in the legs and back but also in the grip. This exercise develops the extensor of the legs and spine, flexors of the arm, elevators of the shoulder girdle and shoulder abductors.

FRONT SQUATS

137

HALTING HIGH DEAD LIFT

138

139

Starting Position. Assume position in (140). The legs are well bent but the back is flat.

Movement. Extend the legs and back vigorously, bringing the arms into action as the bells pass the knees, finishing in the position in (141).

Breathing. Breathe in as you lift and out as you lower the bells to the starting position.

Purpose. To develop all-round body power.

SQUAT BALANCE PRESS

Starting Position. Assume the position as in (142), making sure that the feet are turned outwards.

Movement. Dip the body by bending both legs to lower the bar a few inches. Immediately rebound from this shallow knee-bend by extending the legs and arms to send the bar upwards. Drop under the weight as in (143), by bending the knees into a Full Squat. It is important to force the knees outwards and to keep the trunk upright.

Breathing. Breathe as freely as possible.

Purpose. To build general power in the legs, body and arms. The exercise will also develop mobility and control, exercise the extensors of the arms and legs, the shoulder flexors and elevators of the shoulder girdle.

POWER CLEANS WITH DUMB-BELLS

140

141

SQUAT BALANCE
PRESS

142

143

Starting Position. Assume the position in (144), making sure you are perfectly balanced before you attempt to make your movement.

Movement. From this position, keeping the feet firmly in the same position, quickly bend and stretch the legs. At the same time drive the barbell slightly forwards and upwards as the weight passes the forehead. Now dip the body by lowering into the position shown in (145).

Note the vertical position of the body and the forward position of the left knee. Try to sit on the forward heel without the rear knee touching the floor.

Breathing. Breathe as freely as possible.

Purpose. To co-ordinate power in the legs, arms and shoulders, to build power and develop balance and control. The Snatch Balance Press will build power in the extensors of the arms and legs, the flexors of the shoulder and the elevators of the shoulder girdle. Note the inward turn of the forward thigh—this throws resistance on the legs from a completely different angle from Front and Back Squats.

JERK BALANCE

Starting Position. Assume the position (146). Make sure that the weight is evenly distributed over both feet and that the trunk is nearly vertical. The bar should lay solidly on the chest.

Movement. Bend both knees quickly, straighten the legs and at the same time drive upwards with the arms and shoulders. As the bar clears the top of the head, dip the body by bending the knee to receive the bar in position (147).

Straighten both legs, then lower to the starting position (146).

Breathing. Breathe in as the bar is driven upwards—from then onwards breathe freely.

Purpose. To assist in the improvement of timing in jerking weights overhead but this is also an excellent exercise for most athletes who want to increase their body power.